# MOTMSDD: The Future of Civic Engagement.

**An introductory understanding of the Metaverse of The Minds Social Direct Democracy (MOTMSDD) Approach. AI, BCI, Quantum & Metaverse.**

**By Dr Israel Carlos Lomovasky**

**About the Book**

**"MOTMSDD: The Future of Civic Engagement"**

**Importance of the Book:** "MOTMSDD: The Future of Civic Engagement" is a pioneering work that introduces readers to the innovative concept of Metaverse Of The Minds Social Direct Democracy. This book is crucial for understanding how the intersection of advanced technologies like brain-computer interfaces, AI, and Quantum Computing can fundamentally transform democratic processes. It addresses the complex challenges and immense potential of this model, offering insightful perspectives on the future of governance, public policy, and societal interaction.

**Target Audience:** This book is designed for a broad audience, including technology enthusiasts, policymakers, academics, students, and anyone interested in the intersection of technology and democracy. Its comprehensive approach makes it an invaluable resource for professionals in the fields of political science, computer science, and public administration, as well as for activists and citizens who are passionate about the future of civic engagement and democratic governance.

**Accessibility of the Book:** "MOTMSDD: The Future of Civic Engagement" is written with clarity and accessibility in mind. It meticulously explains complex concepts and provides a glossary of key terms, making it approachable for readers with diverse backgrounds. The book also includes appendices with additional resources, inviting readers to delve deeper into the subjects of digital democracy and technological advancements.

**Conclusion:** This book is more than just a read; it's a roadmap to a future where technology empowers democracy, and every individual has a voice. "MOTMSDD: The Future of Civic Engagement" is an essential guide for anyone looking to understand and shape the future of civic participation in an increasingly digital world.

## Table Of Contents

### Preface

- **Introduction to MOTMSDD**: Present an overview of the concept as envisioned by Israel Lomovasky.
- **Purpose of the Book**: Explain the book's aim to explore and elucidate the principles and potential of MOTMSDD.

### Chapter 1: The Digital Era of Civic Engagement

- **Evolution of Democracy**: Trace the historical development of democratic models leading to the idea of MOTMSDD.
- **The Digital Transformation**: Discuss the role of digital technologies in reshaping societal interactions.

### Chapter 2: The Foundations of MOTMSDD

- **Digital Twin Representation**: Explain how each individual in the MOTMSDD metaverse has a digital twin, representing their personal data and preferences.
- **Direct Democracy Reimagined**: Contrast traditional representative democracy with the direct, real-time participation enabled by MOTMSDD.

## Chapter 3: Technology at the Heart of MOTMSDD

- **Brain-Computer Interfaces (BCI)**: Detail how BCIs facilitate the interconnection between individuals and the digital metaverse.
- **AI, Machine Learning, and Quantum Computing**: Discuss these technologies' roles in analysing data and supporting decision-making in MOTMSDD.

## Chapter 4: Holistic Welfare and Societal Decisions

- **MOTMSDD's Approach to Welfare**: Describe the focus on addressing individual needs over optimizing a theoretical public utility.
- **Public Policy in MOTMSDD**: Explore how MOTMSDD resolves conflicts between citizens' needs through technology, moving away from traditional cost-benefit analysis and Pareto optimality.

## Chapter 5: Envisioning a MOTMSDD World

- **Real-time Democracy in Action**: Provide hypothetical scenarios of MOTMSDD facilitating societal decisions.
- **Impact on Governance and Society**: Speculate on the changes MOTMSDD might bring in governance structures and societal dynamics.

## Chapter 6: Challenges and Considerations

- **Addressing Ethical and Privacy Concerns**: Discuss potential issues related to data privacy, ethics, and the digital divide.
- **Implementation Challenges**: Consider the practicalities and obstacles in realizing the MOTMSDD vision.

## Chapter 7: Preparing for a MOTMSDD Future

- **The Road Ahead**: Discuss steps and strategies for moving towards a MOTMSDD-based society.
- **The Role of Individuals and Communities**: Emphasize how people can engage with and contribute to the development of MOTMSDD.

## Conclusion

- **Recap and Final Thoughts**: Summarize key insights and the transformative potential of MOTMSDD.
- **Call to Action**: Encourage readers to think critically and engage with the ideas presented.

## Appendices

- **Glossary of Key Terms**: Define specific terms and concepts used in the book.
- **Additional Resources**: Suggest further readings for those interested in exploring MOTMSDD in more depth.

This table of contents aims to provide a comprehensive and engaging exploration of MOTMSDD, tailored to readers interested in the intersection of technology, democracy, and societal governance. It seeks to present the concept in a manner that is both informative and thought-provoking, encouraging readers to contemplate the future of civic engagement in a digitally augmented world.

The MOTMSDD, or **Metaverse Of The Minds Social Direct Democracy**, as presented in the provided context, represents a forward-thinking and revolutionary approach to governance and societal decision-making by integrating advanced technologies with democratic principles.

**MOTMSDD Explained:**

In a world increasingly connected and augmented by digital experiences, the MOTMSDD envisions a scenario where every citizen is interconnected through a brain-computer interface (BCI) to a digital metaverse. This isn't just any digital realm; it's a space where ideas, desires, needs, and preferences of individuals are continuously mapped, analysed, and represented.

**Key Features of MOTMSDD:**

1. **Digital Twin Representation**: In the MOTMSDD metaverse, every individual has a digital twin. This twin embodies all relevant data about a person, from their basic needs and preferences to more complex socio-economic and personal data. It serves as a digital delegate, voicing the individual's views, desires, and needs.
2. **Direct Democracy**: Traditional democracy often relies on representative models where elected officials make decisions on behalf of the masses. MOTMSDD, on the

other hand, empowers each citizen to have a direct say in public decision-making processes. With BCIs and the digital metaverse, voting on policies, regulations, or societal changes can be done in real-time, ensuring that everyone's voice is heard instantly and authentically.

3. **Harnessing Technology**: At the core of MOTMSDD lies the intricate integration of several cutting-edge technologies. BCIs bridge the gap between neural activity and digital input, AI and Machine Learning analyse vast amounts of data for efficient decision-making, and quantum computing offers computational power that is unparalleled.

4. **Holistic Welfare**: The ultimate aim of MOTMSDD is to ensure genuine public welfare. With a system that captures every individual's needs and desires accurately, policy decisions can be tailor-made to benefit the broader society while respecting individual preferences and rights.

In essence, the concept of MOTMSDD, as introduced by Israel Lomovasky, seeks to leverage technology's immense potential to revolutionize the democratic process. It represents a blend of the individualistic essence of democracy with the collective power of technology, aiming for a future where everyone's voice not only matters but is also actively integrated into the societal fabric.

In the framework of MOTMSDD public policy decisions are taken by resolving the conflicts between citizens true needs and not as the classical cost benefit analysis using among other techniques the pareto optimality which optimise a theoretical public interest utility function.

In a MOTMSDD world, satisfying needs and not optimising public utility(which does not really exist) is the way to go.

**About the author**

**Curriculum Vitae**

**Education:**

- Doctor of Science (DSc) in Project Evaluation, Technion, Haifa, Israel
- Master of Science (MSc) in Operations Research, London School of Economics
- Bachelor of Science (BSc) in Industrial and Management Engineering, Technion, Haifa, Israel

**Teaching and Academic Research Positions Held:**

- Micro Economics
- Macro Economics
- Econometrics
- Statistics
- Mathematics
- Public Finance
- Urban Planning Mathematical Models
- Transportation Science

**Urban and Regional Planning Experience:**

- Comprehensive Urban Renewal Project Manager (Physical and Social Project) of the East Acco Government Project. Received the title Yakir Acco from the Acco municipality.

## Mathematical Modelling Projects:

- Optimal production mix model using linear programming for the Israeli Paper Mill, Hedera.
- Optimal loading and unloading of ships in Ashdod port using mathematical simulation and integer programming models for the Phosphates at the Negev company.
- Optimal mining order for the Phosphates at the Negev company using mathematical linear, integer, and nonlinear programming.
- Optimal ship operation to transport crude oil using a simulation model for the Institute of By Sea Transport at Haifa.
- Traffic assignment mathematical model for the Transportation Science Institute, Technion, Haifa.
- Industrial Land use analysis in the city of Tel Aviv using Principal Factors Analysis for Tel Aviv Municipality.
- Pupils distribution among the Tel Aviv school system using an integer programming model for the Municipality of Tel Aviv.
- Various mathematical programming models for El Al, The Electric Company, Teva, etc., in association with the Representative of SAS in Israel (Maia Computers).
- Truck fleet routing model based on mathematical programming and heuristics models for international clientele.

- Optimal Locomotive and personnel assignment (run cutting problem) to trains using integer programming models for the New York City Transit Authority.
- Statistical analysis for sales for the American Cyanamid company in Pearl River, New Jersey.
- Sales analysis models (econometric and statistical models) for JC Penny, USA.

**Professional Experience:**

- Founding partner (2006-2011) in the company "Kaul and Lomovasky Holdings Inc" specializing in the computerization of trading using artificial intelligence.
- Internet and Artificial Intelligence Programmer, Developer, and Consultant (2012-2018).
- Developed an AI-based system to calculate the price of apartments in 300 towns in Israel, using VBA Excel Neural Networks (artificial intelligence) pre-processing and presented the prices on a Python Django-based website.
- Author of several books on topics such as algorithmic trading, quantum computing, crypto trading, artificial intelligence, and startup ideas.

**Computer Programming Skills:**

- C, VBA under Excel, Microsoft Office, HTML, PHP, MATLAB, SAS, Python, Django, Keras, Panda, Cloud AI Applications, TensorFlow, Google Cloud Platform, OpenCV, Adversarial GANs, Computer Vision, Image Classification, Object Recognition, Pose Recognition.
- Quantum computing and quantum machine learning.
- Algorithm development, end-to-end ownership.

**Publications:**

- List of books published from 2018 to 2023 covering topics such as algorithmic trading, quantum computing, artificial intelligence, futurology, and startup ideas.

ALGORITHMIC TRADING FROM SCRATCH TO AI/ML STRATEGIES IMPLEMENTED IN PYTHON.FOR CRYPTO,STOCKS,FOREX AND MORE.: RETAIL TRADING SYSTEMS FROM BASIC TO SOPHISTICATED ... STEP BY STEP. PYTHON FOR YOUR PROJECTS

-QUANTUM COMPUTING AND OPERATIONS RESEARCH.AN PART.WHAT IS QC AND WHY IT MATTERS TO OR PRACTITIONERS.: THE FUTURE IMPLICATIONS OF QUANTUM COMPUTING ON OPTIMIZATION AND OPERATIONS RESEARCH

-CRYPTO TRADING TECHNICAL ANALYSIS: Apply the technical analysis indicators, time-frames and approaches that fit Crypto Currencies trading characteristics.

-ALGORITHMIC TRADING STRATEGIES AND TECHNIQUES IN PYTHON, PSEUDO-CODE AND TRADESTATION CODE.: Get your projects started.20 most used techniques and strategies covering all tradeable assets.

-QUANTUM MACHINE LEARNING: A COMPREHENSIVE GUIDE WITH PRACTICAL EXAMPLES AND QUANTUM LANGUAGE IMPLEMENTATION: FROM BASICS TO ADVANCED.INCLUDES PYTHON CODE. (Quantum Computing)

-ALIEN CONSCIOUSNESS UNVEILED: MIND WRITING, MIND CONTROL AND COEXISTENCE: APPLYING SCIENTIFIC METHODS TO STUDY A SCIENCE FICTION QUESTION WITH PHILOSOPHICAL IMPLICATIONS.

-THE BIG LIST OF AI AND ML BUSINESS STARTUP IDEAS.FIND YOUR NICHE.: Artificial Intelligence/Machine Learning : 43 Fields and Over1000 Startup Ideas

-Future social, political and economic revolution of the metaverse of the minds (MOTM) : The communication impact of brain to computer interface. (The future ... and Brain Computer Interface Book 1)

-CRYPTO BASICS TO ADVANCED. MAKE MONEY WITH CRYPTO.THE CRYPTO BUSINESS STARTUP BIBLE.: Investing ,trading and beyond. 20 Cryptocurrency profitable strategies. Over 100 startup ideas

-CRYPTO SENTIMENT ALGO TRADING.PYTHON AND PSEUDO-CODE.: Algo Cryptocurrencies Trade: day, trend, news, swing, arbitrage, bots, contrarian, volume, event, seasonal ,and more strategies.

-THE BIG LIST OF STARTUP IDEAS FOR 2023.: Find Your Niche Among 44 Fields and Over 400 Startup Ideas (Find Your Niche: Business Startup Ideas Book 1)

-THE BIG LIST OF STARTUP IDEAS FOR AFRICA: Find Your Niche Among 33 fields and over 600 Startup Ideas (Find Your Niche: Business Startup Ideas Book 4)

-Business Startup Idea to Living Business. I have a great idea. What's Next.: Materializing your dreams explained in detail with many examples.

-The Metaverse Of The Minds Social Direct Democracy (MOTMSDD): The future of Social Democracy, metaverse and brain computer interface (The future implications ... and Brain Computer Interface Book 4)

-MOTMSDD Urbanism:Redefining Cities through AI and Metaverse of the Minds Social Direct Democracy: Sustainable Urbanism in the Age of Brain-Computer Interface.Solving Conflicts between Citizen's Needs

-Python for Smart Cities: Machine Learning and Artificial Intelligence Applications for Urban Planning and Infrastructure: Python in Action: ML/AI for Smart ... Infrastructure Management (URBANISM Book 2)

-MOTMSDD: Metaverse Of The Minds Social Direct Democracy: Governance and Public Decision Making in The Era of Brain Computer Interface, AI and Metaverse, ... and Brain Computer Interface Book 5

---

## Preface

### *Section 1: Welcome to the Future of Civic Engagement*
**Setting the Scene:**

Imagine a world where every individual has a voice that is not lost in the cacophony of the masses, a world where the lines between the human mind and digital reality blur to create a seamless interface for civic engagement. This is not a distant utopia but a foreseeable future shaped by the rapid evolution of technology and its interplay with the foundations of democracy. Today, we find ourselves at a pivotal moment in the journey of civic engagement. The digital era has unfurled new avenues for communication, transformed how we access and disseminate information, and redefined our interaction with the governing structures. However, despite these advancements, the essence of civic participation – the direct involvement of individuals in decision-making processes that affect their lives – often remains elusive in the traditional democratic setup.

The digital era has undoubtedly brought us closer, but it has also presented new challenges: data overload, privacy concerns, and an increasing sense of disconnect in a hyper-connected world. While social media platforms and digital forums have opened doors for wider participation, they often fall short in translating this participation into tangible and meaningful societal changes. There's a growing sense of urgency to reimagine and revitalize the mechanisms of civic engagement to keep pace with the technological and societal transformations of our time.

**Introducing the Concept:**

In this context, the concept of Metaverse Of The Minds Social Direct Democracy (MOTMSDD) emerges as a groundbreaking approach that promises to bridge the gap between technological advancements and democratic principles.

MOTMSDD is not merely a theoretical construct but a visionary fusion of several cutting-edge technologies – each playing a crucial role in shaping a new paradigm of civic engagement.

At the core of MOTMSDD lies the integration of the Metaverse – a collective, virtual, shared space that is created by the convergence of virtually enhanced physical reality, augmented reality (AR), and the internet. This digital realm becomes the platform where individual voices and opinions are not only heard but are also visualized and quantified. Each citizen is represented by a digital twin in this metaverse, a virtual avatar that embodies all their personal data, opinions, needs, and preferences. This digital twin acts as more than a mere digital representation; it is an active participant in the decision-making processes, ensuring that each individual's views are accurately and consistently represented.

The connection between the individual and their digital twin is facilitated by Brain-Computer Interfaces (BCI), which allow for direct communication between the human brain and external devices. BCIs in MOTMSDD are not just tools for interaction but are integral in creating a seamless and intuitive bridge between thought and digital expression. They enable individuals to interact with the metaverse in real-time, ensuring that their thoughts, opinions, and decisions are instantly reflected in their digital twins.

To process the vast amounts of data generated through these interactions, MOTMSDD harnesses the power of Artificial Intelligence (AI) and Quantum Computing. AI algorithms play a crucial role in analysing and interpreting the complex data sets, drawing insights that inform public decision-making processes. Quantum computing, with its unparalleled computational power, addresses the challenges of processing and managing the massive data influx in the metaverse, making real-time analysis and decision-making feasible.

MOTMSDD represents a paradigm shift from the traditional models of civic engagement. It transcends the limitations of physical and temporal boundaries, bringing about a form of direct democracy that is dynamic, inclusive, and responsive. As we delve deeper into this book, we will explore each component of MOTMSDD in detail, unravelling how this synergistic integration of technology and democracy could potentially redefine our societal structures and governance models. Welcome to a journey into the future of civic engagement – a future where technology empowers democracy, and every voice finds its resonance in the digital symphony of the metaverse.

### Section 2: Introduction to MOTMSDD
### Origins of the Concept:

The genesis of Metaverse Of The Minds Social Direct Democracy (MOTMSDD) can be traced back to the work of Israel Lomovasky. Recognizing the unprecedented pace at which technology was reshaping human interactions and societal structures, Lomovasky envisioned a framework that could harness these technological advancements to fundamentally enhance democratic processes. His concept was not just a response to the emerging digital age but a proactive blueprint for a future where technology and democracy exist in a harmonious and mutually beneficial relationship.

Lomovasky's idea was to create a system that transcended traditional democratic mechanisms, which often struggled to keep up with the rapid changes and challenges of the modern world.

**Defining MOTMSDD:**

At its core, MOTMSDD is a revolutionary approach that synergistically combines the Metaverse, Brain-Computer Interfaces (BCI), Artificial Intelligence (AI), and Quantum Computing to redefine civic engagement and governance. It is a system where every citizen is connected to a digital twin in the metaverse through BCI, creating a dynamic and responsive model of governance that is driven by direct and continuous participation of the populace. This digital twin is not just a representation; it is an active, data-driven entity that reflects the individual's needs, opinions, and preferences. MOTMSDD is thus a leap forward from traditional democracy – it is a direct democracy realized through the power of advanced technology, ensuring that every voice is heard and accounted for in the public decision-making process.

**Components of MOTMSDD:**

The MOTMSDD framework comprises several interlinked components:

1. **Digital Twin Representation**: Each citizen has a digital twin in the metaverse. This twin is a comprehensive digital representation that carries real-time data about the individual, ranging from basic personal preferences to complex socio-political opinions.

2. **Direct Democracy**: Unlike conventional representative democracy, MOTMSDD facilitates direct participation of citizens in governance. Through the metaverse and BCIs, individuals can directly vote on policies and societal changes, ensuring a truly democratic process where decisions are made based on the collective will of the populace.

3. **Harnessing Technology**: At the heart of MOTMSDD lies the intricate integration of cutting-edge technologies. BCIs serve as the bridge between the human mind and the digital twin, enabling seamless interaction and communication. AI and Machine Learning algorithms process and analyse the vast amounts of data generated, while Quantum Computing provides the necessary computational power to handle these complex tasks efficiently.

4. **Holistic Welfare**: The overarching aim of MOTMSDD is to achieve genuine public welfare. Policies and decisions are made based on accurately captured individual needs and desires, allowing for tailored solutions that benefit the wider society while respecting personal rights and preferences.

**The Metaverse and BCI:**

The Metaverse in MOTMSDD is more than a virtual space; it is the foundation upon which the digital twins exist and interact. It is a collective, shared digital reality where individual preferences and opinions are not only expressed but visualized and quantified. The role of Brain-Computer Interfaces (BCI) in this framework is pivotal. BCIs enable direct communication of thoughts and decisions from the individual to their digital twin, ensuring real-time representation and participation. This technology marks a significant leap from conventional methods of communication and interaction in the democratic process, offering a more intuitive and immediate way for citizens to engage in governance.

In this book, we will delve into each of these components in detail, exploring how they come together to form the innovative and transformative concept of MOTMSDD. Through this exploration, we aim to provide a comprehensive understanding of how MOTMSDD can revolutionize civic engagement, making it more inclusive, responsive, and reflective of the true will of the people.

### *Section 3: Purpose of the Book*
**Exploration and Elucidation:**

This book is dedicated to an in-depth exploration of Metaverse Of The Minds Social Direct Democracy (MOTMSDD), a concept at the frontier of integrating advanced technology with the principles of democracy. Our journey through the pages is designed to elucidate the complex mechanisms underlying MOTMSDD, unravelling how it combines the Metaverse, Brain-Computer Interfaces (BCI), Artificial Intelligence (AI), and Quantum Computing to create a novel approach to governance and civic engagement.

In particular, we will delve into the intricacies of how every citizen, connected to their digital twin in the metaverse through BCI, can actively participate in public decision-making. This book aims to shed light on the nuances of this data-driven democracy, where individual needs, opinions, and preferences, encapsulated in the digital twin, inform and influence societal decisions through AI and quantum computing. We will navigate through the theoretical foundations of MOTMSDD, dissect its potential applications, and discuss its far-reaching implications.

**Target Audience:**

"MOTMSDD: The Future of Civic Engagement" is crafted for a diverse audience. It is a valuable resource for policymakers seeking innovative approaches to governance, technologists exploring the intersection of advanced computing and societal applications, and students delving into the fields of political science, computer science, and social studies. Furthermore, this book is an enlightening read for general readers with an interest in the future of governance and how technology can reshape our democratic landscape. Whether you are a professional in the field, an academic, or simply a curious mind, this book offers insights and perspectives that will challenge and expand your understanding of civic engagement in the digital age.

**What to Expect:**

As you embark on this journey, expect to engage with a blend of theoretical discussions, practical insights, and speculative scenarios. The book is structured to guide you through the conceptual underpinnings of MOTMSDD, starting from the basics of the digital twin concept in the metaverse to the sophisticated workings of brain-computer interfaces and their role in real-time democratic participation. You will encounter detailed analyses of how AI and quantum computing are employed to process and utilize the vast amounts of data generated in this digital democracy.

In addition to theoretical exploration, the book presents potential applications of MOTMSDD in various societal contexts, offering a glimpse into what the future of governance could look like. We will also venture into speculative scenarios, painting pictures of how MOTMSDD could transform our societal structures, address contemporary challenges, and present new opportunities for civic engagement.

In summary, "MOTMSDD: The Future of Civic Engagement" is a comprehensive guide to understanding and envisioning a future where technology and democracy converge to create a more inclusive, responsive, and participatory society. Through detailed explanations, examples, and step-by-step analyses, this book invites you to not only understand but also engage with and contribute to the evolving landscape of civic engagement.

### Section 4: The Relevance of MOTMSDD Today
**Contemporary Significance:**

In today's fast-paced, technology-driven world, the relevance of Metaverse Of The Minds Social Direct Democracy (MOTMSDD) cannot be overstated. As we grapple with the vast and ever-expanding digital landscape, traditional models of governance and civic engagement are being challenged by the speed, complexity, and scale of digital communication. MOTMSDD emerges as a timely response to these challenges, proposing a harmonious integration of cutting-edge technology with the democratic process.

The concept of MOTMSDD resonates profoundly in our current era, where digitalization has permeated almost every aspect of our lives. The surge in online platforms has dramatically altered how we interact, form opinions, and participate in societal discourse. However, this digital evolution has also revealed gaps in our current democratic frameworks – gaps that MOTMSDD aims to bridge. By embedding the principles of direct democracy within a technologically advanced metaverse, MOTMSDD promises a more engaged, responsive, and inclusive form of governance, tailored to the digital age.

**Challenges in Current Governance Models:**

Contemporary democratic models, while robust, often struggle with issues like low voter turnout, political polarization, and the slow pace of decision-making. The representative nature of these models sometimes leads to a disconnect between the will of the people and the actions of their elected officials. Moreover, the burgeoning influence of social media and digital platforms, while enhancing connectivity, has also raised concerns about misinformation, echo chambers, and the quality of public discourse.

MOTMSDD addresses these challenges head-on. By leveraging technology to facilitate real-time, informed participation from a broader demographic, it reinvigorates the democratic process. The digital twin concept within the metaverse ensures that each citizen's voice is continuously and accurately represented, circumventing the limitations of traditional polling and voting mechanisms. This approach not only enhances engagement but also fosters a more direct link between the populace and policy outcomes.

**The Role of Technology in Society:**

The role of technology in modern society has evolved from being a mere facilitator of tasks to a fundamental architect of our social, economic, and political landscapes. The advent of AI, quantum computing, and BCIs represents a leap forward in our capability to process information, understand complex patterns, and make informed decisions. These technologies have the potential to redefine the mechanics of governance and public participation.

In the context of MOTMSDD, technology acts as a bridge between individual citizens and the collective societal framework. BCIs allow for a more natural and direct form of communication and expression of opinions, AI and machine learning provide the tools for analysing vast datasets of public opinion, and quantum computing offers unprecedented processing power to manage this complex system. Together, they create a synergy where technology not only supports but actively enhances democratic participation.

In sum, MOTMSDD stands as a beacon of possibility in our journey towards a more participatory and technologically integrated form of governance. It invites us to reimagine the relationship between the individual, technology, and the state, promising a future where democratic engagement is not just a duty, but a seamless, integral part of our digital lives.

*Section 5: Navigating the Book*
**Overview of Chapters:**

As you embark on this exploratory journey through "MOTMSDD: The Future of Civic Engagement," you will traverse through a series of thoughtfully crafted chapters, each contributing a unique perspective to your understanding of MOTMSDD.

- **Chapter 1: The Digital Era of Civic Engagement** sets the stage by exploring the evolution of democracy and the transformative impact of digital technologies on societal interactions. It provides a historical context, highlighting how digital advancements have reshaped the landscape of civic participation.
- **Chapter 2: The Foundations of MOTMSDD** dives into the conceptual bedrock of MOTMSDD. It details the innovative integration of digital twin representation with the principles of direct democracy, underscored by the pioneering use of cutting-edge technologies. This chapter lays the groundwork for understanding the intricate components that constitute the MOTMSDD framework.
- **Chapter 3: Technology at the Heart of MOTMSDD** focuses on the technological pillars of MOTMSDD - Brain-Computer Interfaces (BCI), Artificial Intelligence (AI), and Quantum Computing. It explains how these technologies interplay to facilitate a unique form of democratic engagement and decision-making.

- **Chapter 4: Holistic Welfare and Societal Decisions** examines how MOTMSDD approaches public welfare and policy-making. It contrasts the traditional methods of governance with the nuanced and individual-centric approach offered by MOTMSDD, demonstrating its potential to resolve societal conflicts and cater to collective needs.
- **Chapter 5: Envisioning a MOTMSDD World** presents speculative scenarios and potential applications of MOTMSDD in various societal contexts. This chapter invites readers to visualize the practical implications and transformative impact of MOTMSDD on governance and daily life.
- **Chapter 6: Challenges and Considerations** addresses the hurdles and ethical considerations inherent in implementing MOTMSDD. It critically examines the obstacles in technology, privacy, and societal acceptance, offering a balanced perspective on the path to realizing MOTMSDD.
- **Chapter 7: Preparing for a MOTMSDD Future** outlines the steps and strategies necessary for transitioning to a society underpinned by MOTMSDD principles. It discusses the roles of individuals, communities, and institutions in fostering this revolutionary change.

Each chapter is an integral piece of the larger puzzle, collectively painting a comprehensive picture of MOTMSDD and its potential to redefine civic engagement in the digital age.

**Invitation to Explore:**

As you navigate through these chapters, you are invited not just to absorb the information presented but to actively engage with it. Contemplate the intricate interplay of technology and democracy, envision the practical applications of these concepts in everyday life, and ponder the challenges and ethical dilemmas they present. This book is more than a source of knowledge—it is a catalyst for thought, a prompt for discussion, and a gateway to a future where every individual is an active participant in the democratic process. Your journey through "MOTMSDD: The Future of Civic Engagement" is not just about understanding a concept; it's about envisioning a new paradigm of participation, governance, and societal development in our increasingly digital world.

### Section 6: Final Remarks
**Personal Reflection:**

As the author of "MOTMSDD: The Future of Civic Engagement," I find myself reflecting on the journey that led to the creation of this book. It has been a journey marked by curiosity, discovery, and, above all, a deep belief in the potential of technology to enhance the democratic process. The inception of this book was rooted in a simple yet profound realization: the world is changing rapidly, and our traditional mechanisms of civic engagement are struggling to keep pace.

When I first had the idea of MOTMSDD, I was captivated by its visionary fusion of advanced technologies with the democratic process. The idea of a digital twin representing every citizen in a metaverse, connected through brain-computer interfaces and empowered by the analytical capabilities of AI and quantum computing, seemed like a leap into the future of governance. It was a future that resonated with promise and potential, a future where technology could bridge the gap between the individual and the collective, enhancing participation and representation in ways previously unimaginable.

Writing this book has been an enlightening experience. It has been a journey through the realms of technology, democracy, and social change. I have delved into the complexities of brain-computer interfaces, the vast potential of AI and quantum computing, and the transformative power of the metaverse. But beyond the technological marvels, the heart of this book lies in its vision for society – a vision of a world where every individual's voice is heard, where democracy is not just a concept but a lived, dynamic reality.

My hope is that this book serves as a beacon, illuminating the path towards a more inclusive, responsive, and participatory form of governance. I envision a future where MOTMSDD is not just a theoretical framework but a tangible reality, positively impacting the way we govern and participate in society. I invite readers to not only engage with the ideas presented but also to ponder their implications, challenge their assumptions, and envision their role in shaping this emerging landscape.

The journey of writing "MOTMSDD: The Future of Civic Engagement" has been one of exploration and discovery, and it is a journey I am now sharing with you, the reader. May this book inspire you, provoke thought, and ignite a conversation about the future of civic engagement in our increasingly digital world. Together, let us embark on this journey towards understanding and shaping the future of democracy.

---

## Chapter 1: The Digital Era of Civic Engagement

### *Section 1: Democracy Through the Ages*
### Beginnings of Democracy:

The story of democracy begins in the ancient city-states of Greece, most notably in Athens around the 5th century BCE. This early form of democracy, fundamentally different from what we know today, was based on the direct participation of citizens in decision-making processes. All eligible citizens had the opportunity to speak up and vote on matters of the state in the public assembly, known as the Ecclesia. This system, though limited in its inclusivity by modern standards, marked the inception of a governance model based on collective decision-making and citizen involvement.

As we journey through history, we observe the evolution of these democratic principles across various civilizations. The Roman Republic, for instance, introduced the concept of elected representatives, while the Magna Carta in medieval England laid the groundwork for constitutional governance, emphasizing the rights of individuals and the limitation of sovereign power.

## Evolving Models:

Over the centuries, democracy continued to evolve and adapt to the changing societal landscapes. The Enlightenment era brought forth new ideas about individual rights and the role of government, significantly influencing democratic thought. These ideas were instrumental in shaping modern democratic systems, as seen in the American and French revolutions.

The 19th and 20th centuries saw the spread of democracy globally, along with significant transformations in its practice. The expansion of suffrage, including the right to vote for women and marginalized groups, marked a pivotal shift towards more inclusive democratic systems. Additionally, the emergence of political parties and the increasing complexity of societal issues led to the evolution of representative democracy, where elected officials act on behalf of their constituents.

## The Concept of Representation:

Representative democracy, as it stands today, differs significantly from its ancient direct form. In modern democracies, citizens elect representatives to make decisions on their behalf, a system that has become necessary due to the scale and complexity of contemporary states. However, this shift from direct to representative democracy has brought its own set of challenges. While it addresses the practical difficulties of large-scale decision-making, it often leads to a sense of disconnect between the populace and policymakers. Citizens may feel that their voices are not directly heard or adequately represented, leading to apathy and disillusionment with the political process.

This historical journey of democracy, from its nascent direct form in ancient Athens to the representative models of today, sets the stage for understanding the significance of Metaverse Of The Minds Social Direct Democracy (MOTMSDD). MOTMSDD emerges as a response to the limitations of current democratic models, blending ancient principles of direct participation with advanced digital technologies. It represents an innovative step in the evolution of democracy, striving to enhance citizen engagement and direct representation in the complex, interconnected world of the 21st century.

### Section 2: The Rise and Challenges of Modern Democracy
**Modern Democratic Challenges:**

In the contemporary landscape, democracy faces a myriad of challenges that test its resilience and adaptability. One of the most pressing issues is voter apathy, a phenomenon where a significant portion of the electorate remains disengaged from the political process. This disengagement often stems from a belief that individual votes do not impact the larger political outcome, leading to lower voter turnout and a weakened democratic process.

Political polarization is another critical challenge. Societies around the world are increasingly divided along ideological lines, often exacerbated by echo chambers in digital and social media. This polarization can lead to a breakdown in constructive dialogue, hindering consensus-building and collaborative governance.

Furthermore, the influence of special interest groups has raised concerns about the integrity and representativeness of democratic processes. Lobbying and campaign financing by these groups can lead to policies that favour a select few, undermining the principle of equality that is fundamental to democracy.

**Global Perspectives:**

The practice of democracy is not uniform across the globe; it varies significantly based on cultural, historical, and social contexts. For instance, Scandinavian countries, known for their high levels of citizen trust in government, have developed robust welfare systems and practices of participatory democracy. In contrast, nations with a history of authoritarian rule may struggle with the establishment and maintenance of democratic institutions.

Emerging democracies, particularly in regions transitioning from non-democratic regimes, face unique challenges such as building democratic institutions, ensuring free and fair elections, and cultivating a democratic culture among citizens. The diverse global perspectives on democracy demonstrate its adaptability and the need for models that reflect the specific needs and contexts of different societies.

**Crisis and Reinvention:**

Democracy has not been a static entity; it has evolved through crises and reinvention. Historical events such as the World Wars, the Civil Rights Movement in the United States, and the fall of the Berlin Wall were pivotal in shaping the democratic landscape. Each crisis brought to light the deficiencies of existing democratic models and prompted innovations and reforms.

For instance, the Civil Rights Movement led to significant legislative changes that addressed racial discrimination and voting rights in the United States. The collapse of the Soviet Union ushered in a wave of democratization across Eastern Europe. These moments of crisis were catalysts for reflection, debate, and ultimately, the evolution of democratic governance.

In today's digital era, democracy is undergoing another phase of transformation. As we confront the challenges of voter apathy, polarization, and the disproportionate influence of special interests, there is a growing need for models like MOTMSDD, which aim to revitalize democratic engagement by integrating advanced technologies. This integration promises to address contemporary challenges by enhancing participation, fostering transparency, and ensuring that the democratic process truly reflects the will and needs of the people.

### Section 3: The Digital Revolution
### Dawn of the Digital Age:

The digital age, often heralded as one of the most significant revolutions in human history, began its ascent with the advent of personal computing and the internet. This era marked a paradigm shift in how information was created, shared, and consumed. It democratized access to information, breaking down geographical and socioeconomic barriers. The impact of this revolution extended beyond the realms of personal communication, deeply influencing society and governance. Governments and institutions worldwide found themselves at a crossroad, where traditional methods of governance and public engagement were challenged by the rapidly evolving digital landscape.

**Digital Technologies and Their Impact:**

Three key technological developments have been instrumental in reshaping our societal fabric: the internet, social media, and mobile technology.

- **The Internet**: Since its inception, the internet has evolved from a niche communication tool to a global platform that connects billions. It has transformed how governments operate, how policies are discussed, and how citizens engage with political processes. The internet has facilitated greater transparency and accountability in governance, allowing for the easy dissemination of public information and fostering more informed citizenry.
- **Social Media**: Platforms like Twitter, Facebook, and Instagram have revolutionized communication, enabling real-time, borderless interactions. Social media has become a powerful tool for political mobilization, advocacy, and grassroots campaigns. It has given rise to citizen journalism, where ordinary individuals can report and disseminate news, sometimes circumventing traditional media channels.
- **Mobile Technology**: The ubiquity of smartphones has further amplified the impact of digital technology. Mobile devices have made digital access more

immediate and personal, allowing people to engage with civic and political issues anytime and anywhere. This constant connectivity has facilitated new forms of civic participation, from online petitions to hashtag activism.

## Digital Participation:

Digital platforms have enabled novel forms of civic engagement and political activism. Examples abound:

- **Online Petitions and Crowdsourcing**: Platforms like Change.org have empowered individuals to start and participate in online petitions, influencing policy decisions and bringing attention to various causes.
- **Social Movements**: Movements like #MeToo and #BlackLivesMatter gained momentum and global attention through social media, demonstrating the power of digital platforms in mobilizing public opinion and driving social change.
- **E-Governance**: Many governments have embraced digital platforms to enhance civic engagement. Initiatives like e-voting, digital public forums for policy discussion, and the use of social media for government communication are examples of how digital participation is being integrated into the fabric of governance.

As we enter deeper into the digital age, these technologies have set the stage for more integrated and advanced systems like MOTMSDD. This evolution signifies a move towards a more connected, responsive, and participatory form of democracy, where the convergence of digital technologies with democratic principles opens up new horizons for civic engagement.

### Section 4: Bridging Democracy and Technology
### Technology as a Democratic Tool:

The intertwining of technology and democracy has opened up new avenues for enhancing democratic processes. In recent years, technology has played a pivotal role in facilitating civic engagement and participation. For instance, online voting systems offer a more accessible and convenient way for citizens to exercise their voting rights, especially for those living in remote areas or for those with mobility issues. Estonia, a leader in digital governance, has successfully implemented e-voting, demonstrating its potential to increase voter turnout and streamline the electoral process.

Another aspect where technology bolsters democracy is through data analytics and big data. Governments and organizations can utilize these tools to gain insights into public opinion, enabling more informed policy-making that aligns with the citizens' needs and preferences. An example of this is the use of open data initiatives, where governments release datasets to the public, fostering transparency and allowing citizens, researchers, and developers to analyse and utilize this information for societal benefit.

### Challenges and Critiques:

However, the marriage of technology and democracy is not without its challenges and criticisms. One significant concern is the issue of misinformation and fake news, which has the potential to distort public opinion and disrupt democratic processes. Social media platforms, while being powerful tools for communication, can also become conduits for the spread of false information, influencing elections and public sentiment.

Another challenge is the digital divide – the gap between those who have access to digital technologies and those who do not. This divide can lead to unequal participation in the democratic process, where those without access or digital literacy are left out of important conversations and decisions.

Privacy concerns also loom large in the digital era. The collection and analysis of large amounts of personal data raise questions about consent, data protection, and the potential for surveillance. This has led to a critical discourse on balancing the benefits of digital tools in governance with the rights and freedoms of individuals.

**Innovations in Digital Governance:**

Despite these challenges, there have been significant innovations in digital governance across the globe. Smart cities like Barcelona and Singapore use technology to enhance public services and citizen engagement. They employ IoT (Internet of Things) sensors and data analytics to improve urban infrastructure, traffic management, and environmental monitoring, making governance more efficient and responsive to the needs of residents.

Participatory budgeting platforms, such as those used in New York City and Porto Alegre, Brazil, allow citizens to decide how a portion of the public budget is spent. These platforms enable direct citizen involvement in financial decision-making, reflecting a more democratic and transparent approach to budget allocation.

As we segue into the concept of MOTMSDD, these examples set the stage for a more advanced integration of technology and democracy. MOTMSDD represents the next step in this evolution, where the metaverse, BCI, AI, and quantum computing converge to create a model of governance that is not only technologically advanced but also deeply democratic and participatory. This model promises to address many of the challenges faced by contemporary democracies, offering a vision of a future where every citizen is actively and effectively engaged in the democratic process.

### *Section 5: Setting the Stage for MOTMSDD*
**From Digital Democracy to MOTMSDD:**

The journey from the concept of digital democracy to the emergence of Metaverse Of The Minds Social Direct Democracy (MOTMSDD) represents a significant leap in the evolution of civic engagement. While digital democracy has paved the way for enhanced participation through online platforms, social media, and e-governance, it has also laid bare the limitations and challenges of integrating technology within democratic processes. Issues like digital divides, misinformation, and the challenge of ensuring meaningful participation in a rapidly evolving digital landscape persist.

Enter MOTMSDD – a concept that transcends the boundaries of digital democracy. It represents an innovative synthesis of the latest technological advancements with the core principles of democracy. MOTMSDD is not merely an extension of digital democracy; it is a reimagining of it, a bold step towards a future where technology does not just support democratic processes but is fundamentally interwoven with them.

**The Need for a New Model:**

The need for a new model like MOTMSDD arises from both societal and technological changes. Societally, there is an increasing demand for more direct and meaningful participation in governance. Citizens today seek greater transparency, accountability, and responsiveness from their governments. They desire a democracy that is not only accessible but also truly representative of their needs and aspirations.

Technologically, the rapid advancements in areas like the Metaverse, Brain-Computer Interfaces (BCI), Artificial Intelligence (AI), and Quantum Computing present unprecedented opportunities to meet these societal demands. These technologies offer the potential to create a more dynamic, interactive, and responsive form of democracy. They can enable real-time participation, enhance decision-making processes with data-driven insights, and foster a deeper sense of connection and engagement among citizens.

**Preview of MOTMSDD:**

MOTMSDD is an embodiment of this new wave of democracy. At its heart lies the concept of a digital twin for every citizen in the metaverse – a virtual representation that contains all pertinent information about an individual, such as their needs, opinions, and preferences. These digital twins are connected to their human counterparts through Brain-Computer Interfaces, ensuring a seamless flow of information and interaction.

AI and Quantum Computing play critical roles in processing the vast amounts of data generated within this system, enabling informed and efficient public decision-making. In a MOTMSDD framework, democracy is no longer confined to periodic voting or limited to interactions with representatives; it becomes an ongoing, living process where every citizen is an active participant.

As we segue into the next chapter, we will delve deeper into the intricacies of MOTMSDD. We will explore how it harnesses the power of advanced technologies to create a more inclusive, transparent, and effective democratic system. MOTMSDD stands as a beacon for the future of civic engagement, promising a more connected and empowered society where every voice matters and every opinion counts.

### Section 6: Reflections and Provocations

As we conclude the first chapter of "MOTMSDD: The Future of Civic Engagement," it is essential to pause and reflect on the journey we have embarked upon. This section is designed not just to summarize what we have explored but to provoke thought and encourage a deeper contemplation of the themes discussed.

**Reflective Questions:**

- How does the evolution of democracy from its ancient origins to its current digital form influence our understanding of civic participation and representation?
- In what ways can the integration of advanced technologies like AI, BCI, and the Metaverse redefine the traditional structures and processes of democracy?
- How might the concept of a digital twin in the Metaverse, representing each citizen's views and needs, change the dynamics of policy-making and governance?
- What are the ethical considerations and potential risks involved in transitioning to a digital democracy model like MOTMSDD, and how might society address these challenges?
- How can the principles of direct democracy be preserved and enhanced in an era dominated by digital technologies and rapid information exchange?

**Implications for the Future:**

The journey into the future of democracy in the digital age, particularly with the advent of MOTMSDD, is fraught with both challenges and opportunities. The potential impact of MOTMSDD on democratic processes is profound. It promises a future where democracy is not just a periodic exercise of voting but a continuous and dynamic interaction between citizens and their government. This model has the potential to create a more responsive, transparent, and inclusive governance system, one that is attuned to the real-time needs and preferences of its citizens.

However, this future also raises critical questions about data privacy, the digital divide, and the integrity of decision-making processes in a highly interconnected digital world. As we advance, it becomes crucial to strike a balance between leveraging technological advancements for the betterment of society and safeguarding the fundamental values and rights that underpin a democratic society.

The potential impact of MOTMSDD extends beyond the realms of governance and politics. It has implications for societal structures, economic models, and cultural norms. The integration of the Metaverse, BCI, AI, and Quantum Computing in the realm of civic engagement could herald a new era of social organization, where the lines between the physical and digital worlds become increasingly blurred, and the collective intelligence of society is harnessed in unprecedented ways.

In this light, "MOTMSDD: The Future of Civic Engagement" is more than just an exploration of a concept; it is a call to reimagine our democratic ideals in the context of the ever-evolving digital landscape. It invites readers, policymakers, technologists, and citizens to participate in shaping this future, to ensure that as we advance technologically, we also progress in creating a society that is more democratic, equitable, and just.

## Chapter 2: The Foundations of MOTMSDD

### Section 1: Introduction to Digital Twins
### Defining Digital Twins:

A digital twin, in its most fundamental form, is a virtual replica of a physical entity. This concept, initially emerging from the fields of manufacturing and urban planning, has rapidly evolved to encompass more complex systems, including human behaviours and societal patterns. In the context of Metaverse Of The Minds Social Direct Democracy (MOTMSDD), a digital twin takes on a more nuanced and dynamic role – it becomes a comprehensive digital representation of an individual citizen within the metaverse. This representation is not static; it is an evolving avatar that continuously updates and reflects the individual's preferences, needs, opinions, and behaviours. The digital twin in MOTMSDD functions as a bridge between the physical person and the digital world, offering a unique medium for interaction and representation in the sphere of governance.

**Historical Development:**

The concept of the digital twin has its roots in the early 2000s, primarily within the aerospace and automotive industries. It was used as a tool for the creation of detailed simulations of physical assets. For instance, in aircraft design and maintenance, digital twins were employed to model and monitor the condition of airplanes in real-time, predicting maintenance needs and enhancing operational efficiency.

As technology progressed, the application of digital twins expanded into urban planning and smart city initiatives. Cities like Singapore have utilized digital twins to model urban environments, enabling city planners to simulate and analyse the impact of various scenarios such as traffic flow, energy consumption, and disaster response strategies.

In the realm of MOTMSDD, the digital twin concept is elevated to encapsulate not just physical or environmental aspects but the very essence of human thought and societal interaction. This evolution represents a significant leap from industrial applications to a more personalized, human-centreed use of technology. In MOTMSDD, digital twins serve as a nexus between the individual citizen and the collective digital society, facilitating a new form of democratic participation and decision-making. They act as real-time, interactive agents within the metaverse, providing a platform for each citizen to have a direct and ongoing input into governance processes.

The progression of digital twins from industrial tools to integral components of a digital democracy highlights the expansive potential of this technology. As we delve deeper into the workings of MOTMSDD, the role of digital twins becomes central to understanding how technology can revolutionize the way we engage with and participate in our societal and governance structures.

### Section 2: Digital Twins in the MOTMSDD Metaverse
**Personal Data and Digital Representation:**

In the MOTMSDD framework, digital twins are far more than mere digital avatars or profiles; they are comprehensive representations of individuals, encompassing a wide range of personal data. These virtual counterparts in the metaverse encapsulate not just basic demographic information but extend to capture intricate details such as personal preferences, behavioural patterns, socio-economic background, and even real-time physiological data. For instance, a digital twin could reflect an individual's stance on various social issues, their response to policy changes, and their everyday interactions within the metaverse.

The richness of data encapsulated in these digital twins is pivotal to the functioning of MOTMSDD. It ensures that every citizen's voice is represented in a multi-dimensional and dynamic manner, transcending the limitations of traditional survey methods or opinion polls. This depth of representation allows for a more nuanced understanding of public needs and preferences, enabling tailored and effective decision-making in governance.

**Functionality and Interactivity:**

The functionality of digital twins in the MOTMSDD metaverse goes beyond passive data representation. These entities are interactive, capable of engaging in the metaverse's digital ecosystem. They interact with policy initiatives, participate in virtual referendums, and engage in dialogues with other digital twins, reflecting their human counterparts' opinions and decisions in real time.

For instance, when a new policy proposal is introduced in the metaverse, digital twins can analyse its implications based on the data they hold and provide feedback or vote on behalf of the individual they represent. This process is not a one-off occurrence but a continuous, dynamic interaction, ensuring that citizens' views are consistently integrated into the decision-making process.

Moreover, digital twins can communicate and collaborate with each other, forming interest groups or coalitions in the metaverse, mirroring the complexities of real-world social and political interactions. This feature of MOTMSDD democratizes policy-making, making it a participatory and inclusive process.

**Ethical Considerations and Privacy:**

The integration of comprehensive personal data within digital twins raises significant ethical considerations and privacy concerns. Ensuring the security and confidentiality of this data is paramount, as any breach could lead to misuse or manipulation of personal information.

In the MOTMSDD framework, strict protocols and advanced encryption methods are employed to protect data integrity and privacy. Moreover, the system is designed to operate on principles of consent and transparency. Individuals have control over what data is shared and can review how their digital twin interacts in the metaverse. This approach aims to strike a balance between the benefits of personalized representation and the imperative of safeguarding individual privacy.

Additionally, ethical guidelines govern the use and management of data within MOTMSDD. These guidelines ensure that data is used responsibly and that the digital representation of individuals aligns with their real-world values and rights. The ethical framework also addresses potential biases in data interpretation and decision-making, striving for a fair and equitable digital democracy.

In summary, digital twins in the MOTMSDD metaverse represent a groundbreaking integration of personal data and digital technology, enabling a new form of dynamic and interactive civic engagement. However, this innovation is accompanied by a commitment to ethical standards and privacy safeguards, ensuring that the digital empowerment of citizens does not come at the cost of their security and autonomy.

### *Section 3: The Evolution of Direct Democracy*
**From Ancient Agoras to Modern Times:**

Direct democracy, where citizens directly participate in decision-making processes, traces its roots back to ancient civilizations, most notably in Athens. In these early forms, citizens would gather in agoras or public spaces to deliberate and vote on laws and policies. This system, while revolutionary, was confined to small populations and was limited to those who were granted citizenship, excluding women, slaves, and foreigners.

As we journey through history, the application of direct democracy has evolved but remained limited in scope due to practical challenges. In medieval and early modern times, direct democratic practices were sporadic, often seen in small communities or specific contexts like the Swiss Landsgemeinde, where citizens would gather annually to vote on local matters.

In contemporary times, direct democracy has taken various forms, such as referendums, plebiscites, and citizens' initiatives. These modern adaptations allow citizens to vote directly on specific issues, bypassing the representative legislative process. However, these mechanisms are usually employed intermittently and often for decisions of significant national or regional importance, such as constitutional amendments or independence referendums.

**Limitations of Traditional Direct Democracy:**

The implementation of direct democracy in contemporary societies faces several challenges:

1. **Logistical and Practical Challenges**: Organizing and conducting direct democratic processes on a large scale is logistically complex and resource-intensive. Collecting and counting votes, ensuring accessibility for all citizens, and managing the process efficiently are significant challenges, especially in large and diverse nations.
2. **Scalability Issues**: Direct democracy works well in small communities or for specific issues but becomes increasingly difficult to manage as the scale increases. The diversity of opinions, the complexity of issues, and the sheer number of participants can make the process cumbersome and slow.
3. **Information Overload**: In today's world, the complexity and technicality of policy matters require specialized knowledge. Expecting citizens to be informed on a wide range of issues for direct voting can lead to information overload and may result in uninformed or superficial decision-making.
4. **Risk of Majority Tyranny**: Direct democracy can sometimes lead to the tyranny of the majority, where the rights and needs of minority groups are overlooked. Ensuring that all voices are heard and considered is a critical challenge in such a system.

In light of these limitations, the MOTMSDD approach proposes a revolutionary solution. By integrating advanced technologies like the Metaverse, BCI, AI, and Quantum Computing, MOTMSDD seeks to overcome the logistical, practical, and scalability challenges of traditional direct democracy. It offers a model where direct participation is continuous, informed, and inclusive, transcending the limitations of conventional methods. This innovative approach revitalizes the concept of direct democracy, adapting it to the demands and possibilities of the 21st century.

.

### Section 4: Direct Democracy in the Age of MOTMSDD Reimagining Participation:

The advent of Metaverse Of The Minds Social Direct Democracy (MOTMSDD) represents a radical shift from traditional representative democracy to a model of direct, real-time participation. While representative democracy delegates decision-making to elected officials, MOTMSDD empowers every individual to have an active role in governance processes. This paradigm shift is enabled by the seamless integration of digital technologies, allowing for a more dynamic and responsive democratic experience.

In traditional systems, citizen engagement often peaks during elections, after which elected representatives make decisions on behalf of their constituents. This model, while effective in managing large populations, can lead to a sense of disconnection between citizens and policy outcomes. MOTMSDD, on the other hand, envisions a continuous and active participation model. Here, the metaverse serves as a virtual public square where every citizen, through their digital twin, can engage in policy discussions, referendums, and decision-making processes on an ongoing basis.

## Mechanics of MOTMSDD Voting and Decision-Making:

The MOTMSDD framework redefines the mechanics of voting and decision-making. Central to this process are the Brain-Computer Interfaces (BCIs) and the digital twins in the metaverse. BCIs enable citizens to communicate their preferences and decisions directly to their digital twins without the intermediary of traditional voting mechanisms. This direct interface allows for real-time expression of opinions and votes on various issues and policies.

For instance, consider a new environmental policy proposed in the MOTMSDD metaverse. Citizens can review, discuss, and vote on this policy through their digital twins, with BCIs translating their thoughts and decisions into digital actions. AI and quantum computing technologies analyse these vast datasets of citizen input, ensuring that the decision-making process is informed, efficient, and reflective of the collective will.

This system not only speeds up the decision-making process but also makes it more transparent and data-driven. Policy outcomes in MOTMSDD are the result of a comprehensive analysis of real-time citizen data, reflecting a true direct democracy model.

## Inclusivity and Empowerment:

One of the core aims of MOTMSDD is to foster a more inclusive and empowered form of civic engagement. By providing each citizen with a digital twin and a direct interface through BCI, barriers to participation such as physical location, mobility, or even time constraints are significantly reduced. This inclusivity ensures that diverse voices, including those of marginalized and minority groups, are heard and considered in the democratic process.

Furthermore, the MOTMSDD model empowers citizens by giving them a continuous and direct role in governance. This empowerment can lead to greater civic responsibility and engagement, as citizens see the direct impact of their participation on policy outcomes. The inclusivity and empowerment fostered by MOTMSDD not only enhance the democratic process but also strengthen the social fabric by ensuring that all citizens have an equal stake in their society's future.

In summary, direct democracy in the age of MOTMSDD reimagines participation, redefines the mechanics of decision-making, and reinforces the principles of inclusivity and empowerment. This innovative approach promises to bring about a more engaged, responsive, and democratic society, where technology serves as a bridge between individual will and collective governance.

### Section 5: Technological Integration in MOTMSDD
**BCIs and AI in MOTMSDD:**

In the MOTMSDD framework, the integration of Brain-Computer Interfaces (BCIs) and Artificial Intelligence (AI) represents a groundbreaking synergy that is pivotal to its functionality. BCIs serve as the direct communication channel between individuals and their digital twins in the metaverse, translating neural signals into digital actions. This interface allows for a real-time, intuitive representation of an individual's thoughts and decisions.

For example, when a citizen contemplates a policy decision, the BCI captures this neural activity and transmits it to their digital twin. This process enables a seamless translation of thought into digital participation without the need for physical interaction, like typing or speaking.

Once these inputs are in the metaverse, AI plays a crucial role in interpreting and acting upon them. AI algorithms analyse the data received from countless digital twins, identifying patterns, preferences, and consensus among the populace. This analysis is not just about aggregating votes or opinions; it involves understanding the nuances of public sentiment and the intricacies of individual preferences. AI in MOTMSDD is tasked with the complex job of making sense of a vast array of human emotions, opinions, and decisions, ensuring that the collective voice is accurately represented in governance decisions.

**The Role of Quantum Computing:**

The massive computational requirements of the MOTMSDD metaverse, with its complex network of digital twins and continuous influx of data, necessitate a level of processing power that is beyond the capabilities of traditional computing. This is where Quantum Computing comes into play.

Quantum Computing operates on the principles of quantum mechanics, allowing it to process large volumes of data at speeds unattainable by classical computers. In the context of MOTMSDD, quantum computers manage the data generated by millions of digital twins, each continuously interacting and making decisions within the metaverse.

The significance of quantum computing in MOTMSDD can be illustrated through the process of policy analysis. When a new policy is proposed, the system needs to rapidly process the reactions of all digital twins, considering not just binary choices but a spectrum of responses and the interconnected implications of these responses. Quantum computing enables this analysis to occur almost instantaneously, providing real-time insights into public opinion and facilitating a dynamic, responsive decision-making process.

In summary, the technological integration in MOTMSDD - the combination of BCIs, AI, and Quantum Computing - creates a sophisticated and powerful framework. This integration allows for a level of civic engagement and governance responsiveness that was previously unattainable. BCIs provide a direct link between the physical and digital realms, AI interprets and acts upon the complex web of data, and Quantum Computing ensures that all of this happens at a speed and scale suitable for real-time governance in the digital age.

- 

### Section 6: Challenges and Opportunities
**Addressing the Challenges:**

The implementation of Metaverse Of The Minds Social Direct Democracy (MOTMSDD) is an ambitious endeavour that faces several challenges.

1. **Technological Barriers**: While the technologies at the core of MOTMSDD – BCIs, AI, and Quantum Computing – have advanced significantly, they are still in developmental stages in terms of widespread practical application. The integration of these technologies to function seamlessly in a complex system like MOTMSDD is a formidable challenge. For instance, making BCIs user-friendly, accurate, and accessible to the general public requires overcoming significant technological hurdles.
2. **Societal Acceptance**: The concept of MOTMSDD, which fundamentally alters traditional democratic processes, may face resistance or scepticism. Introducing a system where decision-making occurs in a digital metaverse, and is heavily reliant on advanced technology, could be daunting for those accustomed to traditional democratic practices. Building trust and understanding among the populace is essential for the acceptance and success of MOTMSDD.
3. **Infrastructural Demands**: The infrastructure required to support a MOTMSDD system is extensive. It involves not just robust digital infrastructure to support the metaverse and data processing but also the physical infrastructure necessary for widespread access to BCIs and reliable internet connectivity. This is particularly challenging in regions with limited technological development.

**Potential Opportunities:**

Despite these challenges, MOTMSDD presents transformative opportunities for governance, civic engagement, and societal welfare.

1. **Enhanced Democratic Participation**: One of the most significant opportunities of MOTMSDD is the enhancement of democratic participation. By allowing citizens to engage directly and continuously with governance processes, MOTMSDD could lead to more democratic societies where policies and decisions are truly reflective of the people's will.
2. **Informed Decision-Making**: The integration of AI and quantum computing in MOTMSDD promises more informed and data-driven decision-making. Policies and governmental actions can be based on comprehensive analysis of real-time data, leading to more effective and impactful governance.
3. **Social Inclusivity**: MOTMSDD has the potential to make democratic participation more inclusive. By removing physical barriers to participation and providing platforms for all voices to be heard, MOTMSDD could lead to more equitable and representative governance structures.
4. **Innovation in Governance**: MOTMSDD represents an innovative approach to governance. It can serve as a model for how technology can be used to enhance democratic processes, setting a precedent for future innovations in the field of governance and civic technology.

In conclusion, while MOTMSDD faces several challenges in its implementation, the opportunities it presents for revolutionizing governance and civic engagement are significant. By addressing these challenges head-on, MOTMSDD has the potential to pave the way for a more inclusive, responsive, and efficient democratic future.

### *Section 7: Conclusion and Transition*

As we conclude this exploration of the foundational concepts underlying Metaverse Of The Minds Social Direct Democracy (MOTMSDD), it's crucial to reflect on the key principles that form the bedrock of this innovative approach to civic engagement.

### Summarizing the Foundations:

MOTMSDD is a visionary framework that integrates advanced digital technologies with the tenets of direct democracy to create a new paradigm in civic engagement. At its core, MOTMSDD leverages the concept of digital twins within a metaverse, connected to the physical individuals through Brain-Computer Interfaces (BCIs). These digital twins represent each citizen's needs, opinions, and preferences, ensuring a continuous and dynamic participation in governance processes.

The role of AI and Quantum Computing is instrumental in interpreting and acting upon the vast amounts of data generated within the MOTMSDD ecosystem. AI algorithms analyse this data to provide insights that inform decision-making, while quantum computing handles the immense computational requirements, allowing for real-time processing and responsiveness.

We delved into the evolution of democracy, from its ancient origins to the present day, and how MOTMSDD builds on these democratic principles to offer a more inclusive, efficient, and representative model. The contrast between traditional representative democracy and the direct, real-time participation facilitated by MOTMSDD underscores a significant shift towards a more engaged and responsive democratic process.

**Transition to Application:**

As we transition from the foundational concepts of MOTMSDD to their practical applications, the next chapter will explore how these principles can be actualized in real-world scenarios. We will delve into the potential applications of digital twins within the metaverse for various aspects of governance and societal decision-making.

The next chapter will provide illustrative scenarios demonstrating how MOTMSDD can transform the way policies are formulated, debated, and implemented. It will explore how this model can address contemporary challenges in governance, such as ensuring transparency, combating misinformation, and fostering a sense of community and shared responsibility among citizens.

We will also consider the practicalities of implementing MOTMSDD in diverse contexts, from local communities to national governments, and how this approach can be adapted to different cultural and societal norms. The potential of MOTMSDD to revolutionize areas such as public policy consultation, urban planning, and social welfare will be examined, offering a glimpse into a future where technology and democracy are seamlessly integrated for the betterment of society.

In essence, the forthcoming chapter promises to transition from the theoretical underpinnings of MOTMSDD to its tangible implications, demonstrating how this pioneering approach can redefine the landscape of civic engagement and governance in the digital age.

---

## Chapter 3: Technology at the Heart of MOTMSDD

### *Section 1: The Role of Brain-Computer Interfaces (BCI)*
### Understanding BCIs:

Brain-Computer Interfaces (BCIs) are systems that enable direct communication between the human brain and external devices. This technology deciphers neural signals, translating them into commands that can interact with computers or machinery. The evolution of BCIs has been remarkable, originating from medical research aimed at assisting individuals with disabilities to broader applications in various fields including gaming, virtual reality, and now, in the realm of civic engagement with MOTMSDD.

The working mechanism of a BCI involves reading brain signals, which are typically captured via electrodes placed on the scalp (non-invasive BCIs) or implanted in the brain (invasive BCIs). These signals are then processed using algorithms that interpret specific patterns as commands. For instance, thinking about moving a hand can be translated into moving a cursor on a computer screen. The advancement in AI and machine learning has significantly enhanced the accuracy and efficiency of these interpretations, making BCIs more responsive and user-friendly.

**BCI and MOTMSDD:**

In the context of MOTMSDD, BCIs serve a pivotal role. They are the primary interface that connects individuals to their digital twins in the metaverse. This connection is crucial for the real-time and direct participation of citizens in the democratic processes within MOTMSDD. Through BCIs, individuals can communicate their thoughts, opinions, and decisions, which are then reflected by their digital twins in the metaverse.

For example, in the decision-making process regarding a new public policy within the MOTMSDD metaverse, a citizen's opinion or vote can be directly transmitted from their brain to their digital twin using BCI technology. This process ensures that the participation is not only instantaneous but also a true reflection of the individual's intent, unfiltered by manual input methods.

**Real-Life Examples and Potential:**

Current BCI technologies have already shown promising applications in various sectors. For instance, in healthcare, BCIs are being used to help people with paralysis regain control over their environments by using their brain signals to operate computers or prosthetic limbs. In the consumer electronics sector, companies are exploring BCIs for gaming and virtual reality, enhancing user experience by integrating thought-based controls.

The potential future developments of BCI technology relevant to MOTMSDD are vast. Advances could lead to more sophisticated and seamless integration, where the interface is not only responsive to conscious thoughts but can also interpret subconscious preferences and inclinations, adding depth to the digital twin's representation. Furthermore, as BCI technology becomes more accessible and non-invasive, its integration into everyday devices could revolutionize how citizens interact with digital platforms and participate in governance.

In summary, BCIs are a cornerstone technology in the MOTMSDD framework, facilitating a direct and profound connection between the physical and digital realms of democracy. As this technology continues to evolve, its potential to transform civic engagement and participation in the digital era becomes increasingly significant.

## Section 2: Interfacing Minds with the Digital World
**The Mechanism of Interaction:**

The integration of Brain-Computer Interfaces (BCIs) in the MOTMSDD ecosystem represents a revolutionary leap in bridging human cognition with the digital world. The process by which BCIs translate neural activity into digital commands is both intricate and fascinating. It involves several key steps:

1. **Signal Acquisition**: BCIs begin by capturing brain signals, typically through electrodes placed on the scalp. These signals are the electrical patterns created by neural activity in the brain.
2. **Signal Processing**: The raw data captured by the electrodes is complex and noisy. Signal processing algorithms are employed to filter and interpret these signals, extracting meaningful patterns from the neural noise.
3. **Command Translation**: Once the signals are processed, they are translated into commands understandable by digital systems. This translation is based on pre-established mappings between specific neural patterns and corresponding commands. For instance, the thought of choosing a particular response in a poll can be mapped to a specific command that registers this choice in the digital twin within the metaverse.
4. **Feedback and Adaptation**: In advanced BCIs, a feedback loop allows the system to learn and adapt to the individual's unique neural patterns. Over time, the BCI becomes more attuned to the user's thought patterns, improving accuracy and responsiveness.

**Challenges and Ethical Considerations:**

Integrating BCIs into daily life, especially in the context of democratic participation and decision-making, brings several challenges and ethical considerations to the forefront.

- **Technical Challenges**: Achieving a high level of accuracy and reliability in translating brain signals to digital commands is a significant technical challenge.

Factors like signal interference, individual variations in brain patterns, and the complexity of deciphering intent from neural activity all present obstacles that need to be overcome for BCIs to be effectively integrated into the MOTMSDD framework.

- **Privacy Concerns**: The use of BCIs raises substantial privacy issues. Brain signals can potentially reveal sensitive personal information, thoughts, or even subconscious biases. Ensuring that this data is securely protected and used only for its intended purpose is paramount. Developing robust encryption methods and secure data handling protocols is essential in safeguarding user privacy.

- **Ethical Considerations**: The ethical implications of BCIs are profound. Questions arise about consent, autonomy, and the potential for manipulation. Users must have full control over what information is shared and how it is used. Moreover, the potential for BCIs to influence decision-making or behaviour, either intentionally or unintentionally, requires careful ethical considerations and safeguards.

- **Accessibility and Equality**: Ensuring that BCI technology is accessible to all, regardless of socio-economic background, is crucial in the MOTMSDD context. The technology should not create a new form of digital divide or favour certain groups over others. Efforts must be made to make BCIs affordable, user-friendly, and adaptable to diverse needs and capabilities.

In conclusion, while BCIs offer a groundbreaking means of interfacing minds with the digital world, particularly in the realm of democratic engagement as envisioned in MOTMSDD, they bring with them a host of technical, privacy, and ethical challenges that must be addressed. The successful integration of BCIs in MOTMSDD will depend on how these challenges are navigated and the establishment of robust frameworks that ensure the technology is used responsibly, ethically, and equitably.

- 

### Section 3: Artificial Intelligence and Machine Learning in MOTMSDD
**AI and ML Basics:**

Artificial Intelligence (AI) and Machine Learning (ML) are at the forefront of technological innovation, driving advancements across numerous fields. AI refers to the simulation of human intelligence in machines programmed to think and learn. It encompasses a range of technologies capable of performing tasks that typically require human intelligence, such as visual perception, speech recognition, decision-making, and language translation.

Machine Learning, a subset of AI, involves the development of algorithms that enable machines to improve their performance over time as they are exposed to more data. Unlike traditional programming, where machines follow explicitly programmed instructions, ML algorithms allow machines to learn and make decisions based on patterns and inferences from data.

**Role in Data Analysis and Decision-Making:**

In the context of MOTMSDD, AI and ML play a crucial role in managing and interpreting the enormous volumes of data generated by digital twins and BCIs. With potentially millions of digital twins continuously generating data on citizen preferences, opinions, and responses, the task of analysing this data to inform policy decisions is monumental.

AI and ML algorithms are adept at sifting through this sea of data, identifying patterns, trends, and correlations that might not be apparent to human analysts. They can detect subtle shifts in public opinion, track the emergence of new issues, and provide insights into the effectiveness of current policies. For instance, an AI system could analyse data from digital twins to gauge public response to a proposed transportation policy, identifying key areas of support and concern among different demographics.

Furthermore, ML algorithms can adapt and refine their analysis over time, becoming more attuned to the nuances of the population's preferences and responses. This adaptive capability ensures that the insights provided are continually updated and relevant, allowing for more responsive and dynamic policy-making.

**Examples of AI and ML in Practice:**

Real-world applications of AI and ML offer a glimpse into their potential within the MOTMSDD framework. For example, in healthcare, AI algorithms analyse patient data to assist in diagnosis and treatment planning. In the financial sector, AI is used to detect fraudulent transactions by identifying patterns that signal suspicious activity.

Similarly, in the realm of public policy, AI and ML could analyse data from digital twins to predict the impact of policy changes on different sectors of society, anticipate future challenges, or model the outcomes of various decision paths. This level of analysis can transform how policies are crafted, moving from a reactive to a proactive stance in governance.

In conclusion, AI and ML are integral to the operation of MOTMSDD, providing the analytical power needed to process and make sense of the vast amounts of data generated within the system. Their ability to learn, adapt, and provide deep insights is essential for the effective functioning of this advanced model of democracy. As AI and ML technologies continue to advance, their role in enhancing and streamlining the decision-making processes within MOTMSDD will only grow in importance.

### Section 4: Quantum Computing: The Powerhouse of MOTMSDD
### Introduction to Quantum Computing:

Quantum computing represents a paradigm shift in our approach to data processing and computation. Diverging from the principles of classical computing, which relies on bits that exist in a state of 0 or 1, quantum computing uses quantum bits, or qubits. These qubits can exist in multiple states simultaneously, thanks to the principles of superposition and entanglement, fundamental aspects of quantum mechanics.

The superposition allows qubits to perform multiple calculations at once, exponentially increasing computing power. Entanglement, another quantum phenomenon, enables qubits that are entangled to be in a correlated state, where the state of one (in terms of position, momentum, spin, etc.) can depend on the state of another, no matter the distance between them. This unique property of qubits provides quantum computers with the ability to process vast amounts of data much more efficiently than classical computers.

**Quantum Computing in Handling Complex Data:**

In the context of the MOTMSDD framework, the role of quantum computing is pivotal, especially in managing the extensive computational requirements. Given the complex nature of data generated by millions of digital twins and their interactions via BCIs, as well as the sophisticated AI algorithms required to analyse this data, the processing power of classical computing systems is insufficient.

Quantum computing addresses this challenge in several ways:

1. **Enhanced Data Processing**: Quantum computers can process the immense volumes of data from digital twins and BCIs much faster than traditional computers. This capability is crucial for real-time data analysis, which is at the heart of MOTMSDD's dynamic decision-making process.
2. **Complex Pattern Recognition**: Quantum computing excels at identifying patterns in large datasets, a task that is central to AI algorithms within MOTMSDD. This ability allows for more accurate predictions and insights, facilitating informed policy-making and governance.
3. **Simulating Complex Systems**: Quantum computers can simulate complex systems more effectively than

classical computers. In MOTMSDD, this can be used to model and predict the outcomes of various policy decisions, considering a multitude of variables and their interactions within the society.

4. **Optimization Problems**: Many governance and policy challenges are essentially optimization problems, which quantum computing is particularly adept at solving. Whether it's allocating resources efficiently or balancing various societal needs, quantum computing can find optimal solutions faster and more effectively.

In summary, quantum computing serves as the powerhouse behind the MOTMSDD framework, providing the computational muscle to handle the intricate and voluminous data involved in this advanced democratic system. Its ability to process, analyse, and derive meaningful insights from this data in real-time makes it an indispensable component of the MOTMSDD ecosystem, enabling a level of governance responsiveness and efficiency that was previously unattainable. As quantum computing technology continues to evolve and mature, its role in enhancing and revolutionizing democratic processes and civic engagement will become increasingly significant.

### Section 5: Integrating Technologies for a Unified System
**Synergy of BCI, AI, and Quantum Computing:**

The Metaverse Of The Minds Social Direct Democracy (MOTMSDD) framework represents a harmonious integration of several cutting-edge technologies - Brain-Computer Interfaces (BCI), Artificial Intelligence (AI), and Quantum

Computing. Each of these technologies plays a crucial role, but it is their synergy that truly powers the MOTMSDD system.

- **BCI as the Interface**: BCIs are the primary interface for individual participation in MOTMSDD. They capture and transmit neural signals from individuals, translating thoughts and intentions into digital commands. This direct neural interaction is fundamental in realizing a form of democracy where participation is not just active but also intuitive and immediate.
- **AI as the Analyser and Interpreter**: AI algorithms take the data from BCIs and process it to extract meaningful insights. They handle the complexities of interpreting human thoughts and preferences, converting them into actionable data within the metaverse. AI's role in MOTMSDD extends beyond data analysis to include predictive modelling, decision support, and even managing the interactions between millions of digital twins.
- **Quantum Computing as the Processing Powerhouse**: Given the vast amount of data generated and the complexity of computations required, Quantum Computing provides the necessary processing power. It enables the MOTMSDD system to operate efficiently and effectively, handling real-time data processing, complex simulations, and optimization tasks that are beyond the capabilities of classical computing.

Together, these technologies create a cohesive and efficient system. BCIs ensure real-time input from citizens; AI processes this input, providing insights and facilitating interactions within the metaverse; and Quantum Computing supports the system with its immense processing capabilities. This integrated approach allows MOTMSDD to function as a dynamic, responsive, and inclusive democratic system.

**Future Prospects and Developments:**

Looking ahead, the future advancements in BCI, AI, and Quantum Computing hold immense potential for enhancing the MOTMSDD model:

- **Advancements in BCI Technology**: Future BCIs may offer more seamless and non-invasive interfaces, potentially integrated into everyday wearables. Increased accuracy in interpreting neural signals could lead to more nuanced and sophisticated forms of digital interaction.
- **AI Evolution**: AI algorithms are expected to become more advanced in natural language processing, emotional intelligence, and ethical decision-making. This would allow AI in MOTMSDD to better understand and represent the complexities of human thought and societal dynamics.
- **Quantum Computing Breakthroughs**: As Quantum Computing matures, we can expect even faster processing speeds and more efficient handling of complex data sets. This will enhance the system's ability to handle the ever-increasing scale and complexity of democratic decision-making processes.

These technological advancements could significantly enhance the MOTMSDD framework, making it more accessible, responsive, and capable of handling the complexities of modern governance. The potential for these technologies to evolve and integrate more deeply provides an optimistic outlook for the future of civic engagement, paving the way for a more engaged, informed, and participatory democratic experience.

### Section 6: Technological Challenges and Solutions
**Overcoming Technical Barriers:**

The implementation of Metaverse Of The Minds Social Direct Democracy (MOTMSDD) is an ambitious technological endeavour that faces several significant challenges. Addressing these challenges is crucial for the successful realization of the MOTMSDD vision.

1. **Complexity in Integration**: One of the primary challenges is integrating diverse technologies such as BCIs, AI, and Quantum Computing into a cohesive system. Each technology comes with its own complexities and ensuring they work in harmony is a significant engineering and computational challenge.
2. **Advancing BCI Technology**: While BCIs have made remarkable progress, making them more user-friendly, accurate, and non-invasive remains a hurdle. Ongoing research is focusing on developing BCIs that can be used comfortably in everyday settings, reducing reliance on bulky and invasive equipment.
3. **Scaling AI and Quantum Computing**: AI algorithms must be scaled to handle the vast amounts of data generated by millions of digital twins. Similarly, Quantum Computing needs to advance to a point where it can reliably support the massive processing requirements of the MOTMSDD framework. Research in

these fields is rapidly evolving, focusing on enhancing scalability, reliability, and processing capabilities.

**Ensuring Accessibility and Inclusivity:**

For MOTMSDD to be truly transformative, it is essential that the technologies underpinning it are accessible and inclusive.

1. **Reducing Costs**: High costs associated with advanced technologies like BCIs and Quantum Computing can be a barrier to widespread adoption. Efforts must be made to reduce costs, possibly through innovations in manufacturing, subsidies, or scalable designs that make the technology more affordable.
2. **User-Friendly Design**: Technologies must be designed with user experience in mind. BCIs, in particular, should be easy to use and understand, accommodating users with varying levels of tech-savviness and abilities. This includes developing intuitive interfaces and ensuring that interaction with the metaverse is straightforward and engaging.
3. **Addressing the Digital Divide**: Bridging the digital divide is crucial in ensuring that MOTMSDD is inclusive. This means not only making the technology accessible but also providing the necessary infrastructure, such as widespread and reliable internet access, and educational programs to improve digital literacy.
4. **Cultural and Ethical Considerations**: The design and implementation of these technologies must consider diverse cultural norms and ethical standards. This includes ensuring that data handling respects privacy norms of different societies and that the system is adaptable to various governance and social structures.

In conclusion, while the technological challenges in implementing MOTMSDD are significant, they are not insurmountable. Ongoing research and development, coupled with a focus on accessibility and inclusivity, are key to overcoming these barriers. By addressing these challenges, MOTMSDD has the potential to revolutionize the way we engage in civic life and participate in democratic processes.

### *Section 7: Conclusion and Forward Look*

As we conclude this exploration into the technological heart of Metaverse Of The Minds Social Direct Democracy (MOTMSDD), it is essential to reflect on the critical role technology plays in enabling this innovative approach to civic engagement and to consider the future trajectory of this model.

### **Recap of Technological Foundations:**

Throughout this chapter, we have delved into the key technologies that form the backbone of MOTMSDD - Brain-Computer Interfaces (BCI), Artificial Intelligence (AI), Quantum Computing, and the Metaverse. Each of these technologies contributes uniquely to the MOTMSDD framework:

- **Brain-Computer Interfaces** bridge the gap between human thought and digital expression, allowing for real-time communication of citizens' preferences and decisions to their digital twins in the metaverse.
- **Artificial Intelligence** plays a crucial role in processing and interpreting the complex data generated by these

interactions, providing insights and aiding in decision-making.

- **Quantum Computing** addresses the immense computational demands of this system, handling the processing of vast amounts of data with speed and efficiency.
- **The Metaverse** serves as the digital ecosystem where these interactions and processes unfold, creating a virtual space for direct and dynamic civic participation.

**Looking Ahead:**

Looking to the future, ongoing advancements in these technologies hold immense potential for further shaping and refining the MOTMSDD model:

- **Advancements in BCI Technology**: Future developments in BCIs could lead to more sophisticated, non-invasive, and user-friendly interfaces. As BCIs become more integrated into daily life, their application in MOTMSDD could become more seamless and intuitive.
- **Evolving AI Capabilities**: AI is continuously advancing in its ability to process complex data sets and provide nuanced insights. Future AI developments could enhance the accuracy and depth of analyses in MOTMSDD, leading to more informed and effective decision-making processes.
- **Quantum Computing Breakthroughs**: As quantum computing technology matures, it will further enhance the capacity to process data in the MOTMSDD framework. This could allow for more complex

simulations and analyses, enabling a deeper understanding of societal dynamics and policy impacts.

- **Expanding the Metaverse**: The metaverse will likely evolve to become more immersive and interactive. This evolution will enhance the experience of civic participation in MOTMSDD, making it more engaging and representative of real-world interactions.

In conclusion, the technologies underpinning MOTMSDD are not static; they are dynamic and evolving. As they continue to advance, they will undoubtedly bring new dimensions to the MOTMSDD framework, enhancing its efficiency, inclusivity, and effectiveness. The future of civic engagement through MOTMSDD is a promising horizon, one that blends the best of technology with the principles of democracy, paving the way for a more engaged, empowered, and responsive societal governance model.

---

## Chapter 4: Holistic Welfare and Societal Decisions

### Section 1: A New Paradigm in Welfare

As we embark on the exploration of Chapter 4, "A New Paradigm in Welfare," it is essential to understand how Metaverse Of The Minds Social Direct Democracy (MOTMSDD) redefines the concept of public welfare. MOTMSDD ushers in a transformative approach, shifting the focus from traditional, often generalized notions of public utility to a more personalized, individual-centric model.

**Redefining Welfare:**

In traditional governance models, welfare policies are typically designed based on broad demographic data, economic trends, and generalized assumptions about public needs. While these approaches have their merits, they often overlook the nuanced differences in individual needs and circumstances. The MOTMSDD model, with its technological underpinnings, offers a paradigm shift in how welfare is conceptualized and delivered.

Holistic welfare in the MOTMSDD context is about recognizing and responding to the diverse, often complex needs of every individual. It is an approach that seeks not only to address the aggregate needs of a population but to ensure that each person's specific requirements are considered. This approach contrasts sharply with traditional models that tend to offer one-size-fits-all solutions, often leading to gaps in welfare delivery.

**Individual Needs in the Forefront:**

The integration of technologies like AI, BCI, and Quantum Computing in MOTMSDD allows for an unprecedented level of personalization in policy-making. Each citizen's digital twin in the metaverse, a comprehensive and dynamic representation of their needs, preferences, and opinions, becomes a key source of input for policy decisions.

For instance, consider a new healthcare policy. In a traditional setting, such a policy might be based on average health needs and access issues of the general population. In contrast, under MOTMSDD, the policy formulation would involve analysing data from millions of digital twins, each reflecting individual health concerns, access barriers, and even preventive healthcare behaviours. This data enables policymakers to design a healthcare system that is not only efficient and equitable but also tailored to address specific health needs across different segments of the population.

Moreover, the real-time feedback mechanism in MOTMSDD, facilitated by BCIs, ensures that policies remain adaptive and responsive. Citizens can continuously communicate their experiences and satisfaction levels with welfare services, allowing for ongoing adjustments and improvements.

In summary, the first section of Chapter 4 delves into how MOTMSDD revolutionizes the concept of welfare, placing individual needs and preferences at the forefront of policy-making. This new paradigm promises a more inclusive, responsive, and effective approach to public welfare, where every citizen's well-being is acknowledged and addressed in a personalized manner. As we proceed further in this chapter, we will explore the practical implications, challenges, and opportunities of implementing this holistic approach to welfare within the MOTMSDD framework.

### Section 2: Digital Twins and Individual Representation
In the Metaverse Of The Minds Social Direct Democracy (MOTMSDD) framework, digital twins serve as the cornerstone

for reimagining individual representation in welfare policies. This section delves into the role of these digital twins in accurately reflecting individual needs and how they facilitate data-driven decisions in welfare.

**Role of Digital Twins in Welfare:**

Digital twins in MOTMSDD are sophisticated digital representations of individuals, mirroring their real-world preferences, needs, and opinions. These virtual counterparts are continuously updated with data from their human counterparts through Brain-Computer Interfaces (BCIs). This constant stream of data ensures that the digital twins are dynamic and reflective of the current state and evolving needs of each individual.

The significance of these digital twins in welfare is profound:

1. **Personalized Representation**: Digital twins enable a level of personalization in policy-making that was previously unattainable. Unlike traditional demographic models that generalize population needs, digital twins provide insights into the specific requirements of each individual.
2. **Dynamic Welfare Needs Assessment**: Digital twins allow for real-time tracking and analysis of welfare needs. For example, changes in an individual's economic status, health indicators, or educational needs are instantly reflected in their digital twin, allowing for a dynamic assessment of welfare requirements.
3. **Enhanced Engagement and Feedback**: Digital twins facilitate a two-way interaction between individuals and policy-makers. Citizens can provide immediate

feedback on welfare services, leading to a more responsive and adaptive welfare system.

**Data-Driven Welfare Decisions:**

The data generated by these digital twins is a goldmine for policy-makers. Utilizing advanced AI and Quantum Computing, the MOTMSDD system can analyse this data to make informed, targeted welfare decisions.

- **Informed Policy Formulation**: By analysing data from millions of digital twins, policy-makers can identify trends, pinpoint areas of need, and design policies that directly address these issues. For instance, if data indicates a rising trend in mental health issues among a certain demographic, targeted mental health services can be designed and deployed efficiently.
- **Tailored Service Delivery**: Data from digital twins enables the customization of welfare services to meet individual needs. This approach ensures that resources are allocated more effectively, and services are more likely to have a positive impact.
- **Predictive Analysis for Proactive Policy-Making**: AI algorithms can use data from digital twins to predict future welfare needs, allowing governments to proactively develop policies and allocate resources. This predictive capability is crucial in tackling emerging social issues before they escalate.

In conclusion, Section 2 of Chapter 4 highlights the transformative role of digital twins in individual representation within the MOTMSDD framework. By enabling a personalized, dynamic, and data-driven approach to welfare, digital twins ensure that individual needs are at the forefront of welfare decisions. This paradigm shift promises a more effective, responsive, and humane welfare system, where every individual's welfare is a priority, and policies are crafted to meet the unique needs of each citizen.

### Section 3: MOTMSDD's Approach to Public Policy

The approach of Metaverse Of The Minds Social Direct Democracy (MOTMSDD) to public policy marks a significant departure from traditional methods. This section explores how MOTMSDD transcends conventional policy-making frameworks, focusing on resolving conflicts and catering to individual needs through advanced technology.

### Beyond Traditional Policy Making:

Traditional public policy-making often relies on cost-benefit analysis and concepts like Pareto optimality, where policies are designed to maximize overall benefit while minimizing disadvantages. However, this approach can sometimes overlook the specific needs and circumstances of various individuals or minority groups, leading to policies that prefer the welfare of the affluent that is a more substantial player in the economy rather than the less affluent which is less involved in the demand of goods and services providing an averaged optimality in a general sense but not necessarily for each segment of society.

MOTMSDD introduces a paradigm shift in this regard:

- **Personalized Policy Analysis**: Instead of a one-size-fits-all approach, MOTMSDD enables a more granular and individualized analysis of policy impact. Through the data collected from digital twins, policy-makers can understand how a proposed policy might affect different individuals and groups, allowing for more nuanced and tailored policy decisions.
- **Dynamic and Adaptive Policies**: In the MOTMSDD framework, policies are not static; they are dynamic and can be adapted as new data becomes available. This flexibility ensures that policies remain relevant and effective in addressing the evolving needs of the population.

**Resolving Conflicts Through Technology:**

In any society, conflicts of interest and needs are inevitable. MOTMSDD utilizes its technological backbone to address and resolve these conflicts:

- **Role of AI in Conflict Resolution**: AI algorithms in MOTMSDD analyse the vast amounts of data from digital twins to identify areas of conflict in public opinion or policy impact. Using sophisticated modelling and predictive analytics, AI can propose solutions or policy modifications that best reconcile these conflicts, aiming for outcomes that cater to the widest range of needs without marginalizing minority voices.When solving problems the MOTMSDD approach follows the principle of needs first and only after everybodies needs have been satisfied, the rest of the public available budget is allocated to fulfil preferences and desires.

- **BCI Facilitated Engagement**: BCIs play a crucial role in capturing real-time responses and opinions from citizens about various policies. This immediate feedback allows for quick adjustments and helps in mediating conflicts as they arise. Citizens can directly express their concerns or approval, and this data is used to continuously refine and adjust policies.
- **Community Engagement and Consensus Building**: MOTMSDD fosters a digital environment where community engagement and consensus-building are central to policy-making. The metaverse provides a platform for citizens to discuss, debate, and collaborate on policy matters, contributing to a more inclusive and participatory approach to governance.

In conclusion, Section 3 of Chapter 4 illustrates how MOTMSDD revolutionizes public policy-making. By moving beyond traditional frameworks and utilizing advanced technologies like AI and BCI, MOTMSDD ensures that policies are not only efficient and beneficial on a broad scale but also sensitive to the diverse needs and preferences of all citizens. This approach represents a more equitable, dynamic, and responsive model of governance, apt for the complexities and challenges of modern societies.

### *Section 4: Case Studies and Hypothetical Scenarios*

This section provides hypothetical case studies to illustrate how the Metaverse Of The Minds Social Direct Democracy (MOTMSDD) approach can uniquely address welfare and policy issues, contrasting it with traditional models to highlight the advantages and potential challenges.

## Case Study 1: Urban Transportation Policy

*Traditional Model*: In a conventional approach, an urban transportation policy might be formulated based on limited public surveys, traffic data, and economic considerations. The policy could result in a new bus route system designed to optimize travel time and reduce congestion.

*MOTMSDD Approach*: Using MOTMSDD, the policy-making process starts with analysing real-time data from the digital twins of all city residents. The system identifies not just traffic patterns, but also individual preferences for travel times, concerns about environmental impact, and accessibility needs. AI and quantum computing analyse this data, proposing a multi-faceted transportation solution that includes not only optimized bus routes but also provisions for bike lanes and electric vehicle charging stations, catering to a broader range of citizen needs.

**Comparative Analysis**: The MOTMSDD approach offers a more comprehensive and personalized solution by considering individual preferences and needs. However, it requires sophisticated technology and data analysis, posing challenges in terms of privacy and data security.

## Case Study 2: Healthcare Reform

*Traditional Model*: A typical healthcare reform might focus on expanding coverage or reducing costs based on demographic health data and economic factors. This approach, while beneficial, might not address specific community health needs or individual health preferences.

*MOTMSDD Approach*: In the MOTMSDD framework, healthcare reform is driven by detailed health data from each citizen's digital twin. This includes not just medical history, but lifestyle preferences, genetic information, and even real-time health monitoring data. AI algorithms process this data to design a healthcare system that includes personalized healthcare plans, preventive care programs tailored to individual risk factors, and community health initiatives targeting specific local health concerns.

**Comparative Analysis**: The MOTMSDD model allows for a more personalized and preventative approach to healthcare, potentially leading to better health outcomes. However, it raises significant questions about data privacy and requires robust systems to protect sensitive health information.

## Case Study 3: Educational Policy

*Traditional Model*: Traditional educational policy might involve standardized curricula development and resource allocation based on average student performance and school needs.

*MOTMSDD Approach*: Using MOTMSDD, educational policies are shaped by comprehensive data from students' digital twins, including learning styles, academic performance, extracurricular interests, and emotional well-being. The policy, formulated using AI analysis, advocates for personalized learning paths, emotional and psychological support systems, and resource allocation based on individual school and student needs.

**Comparative Analysis**: While the MOTMSDD approach can lead to more personalized and effective education systems, it requires a high level of technology integration in schools and continuous data collection, which could be resource-intensive and raise concerns about student data privacy.

In conclusion, these hypothetical scenarios demonstrate how MOTMSDD could lead to more nuanced, personalized, and effective welfare policies compared to traditional models. While offering significant advantages in terms of personalization and responsiveness, the MOTMSDD approach also brings forth challenges related to technological infrastructure, data privacy, and ethical considerations. These case studies highlight the potential of MOTMSDD to transform policy-making, making it more adaptive to individual and societal needs.

### *Section 5: The Decision-Making Process in MOTMSDD*
**Real-Time Decision Making:**

One of the most revolutionary aspects of Metaverse Of The Minds Social Direct Democracy (MOTMSDD) is its capability for real-time decision-making. This dynamic process is made possible by the seamless integration of advanced technologies – Brain-Computer Interfaces (BCIs), Artificial Intelligence (AI), Quantum Computing, and the Metaverse.

- **Instantaneous Input through BCIs**: BCIs allow for immediate communication of citizens' thoughts and preferences to their digital twins. This direct and instant transmission of data means that people's opinions on various issues and policies can be registered and analysed in real-time, without delays inherent in traditional decision-making processes.

- **Rapid Data Analysis with AI and Quantum Computing**: AI algorithms play a crucial role in swiftly analysing the large volumes of data generated by digital twins. Quantum Computing further enhances this process with its superior processing power, enabling the system to handle complex computations at unprecedented speeds. This combination allows MOTMSDD to synthesize and interpret citizen data quickly, leading to faster decision-making.
- **Responsive Policy Adjustments**: The real-time nature of MOTMSDD enables policies to be adjusted and refined as new data is received. This adaptability ensures that policies remain relevant and effective in addressing the changing needs and opinions of the population.

**Transparency and Accountability:**

Transparency and accountability are key pillars of the decision-making process in MOTMSDD, ensuring that the system remains democratic and trustworthy.

- **Visibility of Decision-Making Processes**: In MOTMSDD, the entire decision-making process, from data collection to policy formulation, is transparent. Citizens can see how their input through digital twins is contributing to decisions, fostering a sense of ownership and trust in the system.
- **Accountability through Data Trails**: The digital nature of MOTMSDD creates a data trail for every decision made. This feature allows for auditing and review

processes, ensuring that decisions are based on accurate data and that any biases or errors can be identified and corrected.

- **Empowering Citizens with Information**: The transparent framework of MOTMSDD empowers citizens with information about how decisions are made, encouraging informed participation. It also holds policymakers accountable, as their decisions are directly based on and influenced by the data-driven voice of the populace.

In summary, Section 5 of Chapter 4 highlights the innovative decision-making process in MOTMSDD, characterized by its real-time nature, transparency, and accountability. This process marks a significant shift from traditional decision-making methods, offering a more dynamic, responsive, and democratic approach to welfare and policy formulation. As we move forward, the potential of MOTMSDD to transform governance and civic engagement becomes increasingly evident, promising a future where technology and democracy synergize to create a more equitable and efficient society.

### Section 6: Challenges and Ethical Considerations
The implementation of Metaverse Of The Minds Social Direct Democracy (MOTMSDD) in welfare and policy comes with a set of unique challenges and ethical considerations. This section explores these issues and offers insights into how they might be navigated.

**Addressing Potential Challenges:**

1. **Data Accuracy and Reliability**: A crucial challenge in MOTMSDD is ensuring the accuracy and reliability of data from digital twins. Incorrect or misleading data can lead to flawed policy decisions. Continuous verification and validation processes must be implemented to ensure data integrity. This might involve cross-referencing data sources and incorporating checks against potential biases or errors in data collection.

2. **Privacy Concerns**: The extensive collection and analysis of personal data in MOTMSDD raise significant privacy concerns. Protecting this data from unauthorized access and misuse is paramount. Robust encryption methods, stringent data access protocols, and clear privacy policies are essential to safeguard individual privacy. Moreover, individuals should have control over what data they share and be informed about how their data is used.

3. **Ethical Implications**: The application of AI in decision-making, especially in welfare and policy, comes with ethical implications. There is a need for ethical frameworks to guide the development and application of AI algorithms, ensuring they are used responsibly and do not perpetuate biases or inequalities. Ethical considerations also extend to the use of BCIs, where the boundary between technology and human cognition must be navigated carefully.

**Navigating Ethical Dilemmas:**

1. **Balancing Individual Rights with Collective Good**: In a system that heavily relies on personal data for public decision-making, striking a balance between individual rights and the collective good is a complex ethical

challenge. Policies must be formulated to ensure that individual rights are not overshadowed by the pursuit of broader societal benefits.

2. **Consent and Autonomy**: Ensuring informed consent and maintaining individual autonomy in the MOTMSDD system is crucial. Users should have a clear understanding of how their data is used and must be able to opt in or out of data-sharing processes. Additionally, the autonomy of individuals in making decisions without undue influence from the system must be preserved.

3. **Addressing Bias and Fairness**: AI algorithms must be scrutinized for biases that could lead to unfair policy outcomes. This involves not only technical solutions to de-bias algorithms but also broader societal efforts to address underlying prejudices that might be reflected in the data.

4. **Transparency and Accountability**: Maintaining transparency in how decisions are made and ensuring accountability for those decisions are vital in navigating ethical dilemmas. This includes clear documentation of decision-making processes and mechanisms for public scrutiny and feedback.

In conclusion, Section 6 of Chapter 4 delves into the complex challenges and ethical considerations inherent in implementing the MOTMSDD approach to welfare and policy. While the potential benefits of this approach are significant, careful attention must be paid to ensuring data accuracy, protecting privacy, and navigating the ethical landscape. Addressing these challenges requires a multifaceted approach, combining technological solutions with robust ethical guidelines and policies.

### Section 7: Conclusion and Implications

As we conclude this exploration of welfare in the context of Metaverse Of The Minds Social Direct Democracy (MOTMSDD), it is essential to recapitulate the vision of this novel approach and consider its broader implications for society, governance, and the future of democracy.

**Summarizing the Vision of Welfare in MOTMSDD:**

MOTMSDD represents a transformative approach to welfare, one that fundamentally rethinks how individual needs and societal welfare are addressed in policy-making:

1. **Personalization of Welfare**: At the core of MOTMSDD is the commitment to personalized welfare, enabled by the comprehensive data from digital twins. This approach ensures that policies are not just shaped by aggregate data but are responsive to the nuanced needs of every individual.
2. **Dynamic and Responsive Policy-Making**: Utilizing the real-time data processing capabilities of AI and Quantum Computing, MOTMSDD fosters a dynamic and adaptive approach to policy-making. This fluidity allows policies to evolve in response to changing needs and preferences, ensuring relevance and efficacy.
3. **Engagement and Empowerment**: MOTMSDD empowers citizens by giving them an active role in the decision-making process. The use of BCIs and the metaverse creates an interactive and inclusive

environment for civic engagement, enhancing the democratic process.

**Broader Implications for Society:**

The implementation of MOTMSDD has far-reaching implications for societal welfare, governance, and the trajectory of democracy:

1. **Transformation of Governance**: MOTMSDD has the potential to revolutionize governance, making it more participatory, transparent, and responsive. This model could lead to greater trust in government and higher satisfaction with public services, as policies are more closely aligned with the public's needs.
2. **Enhanced Societal Welfare**: By focusing on individual needs, MOTMSDD promises a more equitable approach to welfare. This could lead to significant improvements in areas like healthcare, education, and social services, with policies that are more effective and impactful.
3. **Evolution of Democracy**: MOTMSDD represents a new phase in the evolution of democracy – one where technology is harnessed to enhance democratic engagement and decision-making. It provides a glimpse into a future where democracy is not just about representation but about active, continuous participation in governance.
4. **Technological and Ethical Advancements**: The implementation of MOTMSDD will drive technological advancements, particularly in BCIs, AI, and Quantum Computing. Concurrently, it will spur discussions and developments in ethical standards, privacy protection,

and data security, which are vital for the responsible use of technology in governance.

In conclusion, Chapter 4 of "MOTMSDD The Future of Civic Engagement" encapsulates a visionary approach to welfare within the MOTMSDD framework. This approach has the potential to redefine how society addresses welfare and decision-making, marking a significant step towards a more personalized, responsive, and democratic future. As technology continues to advance, the MOTMSDD model offers a template for harnessing these advancements for the greater good, promising a future where technology and democracy synergize to enhance societal welfare and individual well-being.

## Chapter 5: Envisioning a MOTMSDD World

### *Section 1: Introduction to a New Reality*
As we embark on Chapter 5 of "MOTMSDD: The Future of Civic Engagement," we step into a new realm of possibilities opened up by Metaverse Of The Minds Social Direct Democracy (MOTMSDD). This chapter sets the stage for a world transformed by the innovative intersection of technology and democracy, painting a vivid picture of how MOTMSDD redefines societal structures, governance, and the very fabric of civic engagement.

### Setting the Stage:

Imagine a world where every citizen is not just a passive recipient of government decisions but an active participant in the decision-making process. In this world, the boundaries between the physical and digital realms blur, as citizens interact with their governments and each other in a dynamic, virtual space. Here, personal preferences, needs, and opinions are not mere statistics in government reports but vital inputs that shape policies in real-time. This is the world of MOTMSDD – a world where democracy is revitalized, and civic engagement is not limited to voting in elections but is a continuous, integrated part of everyday life.

In this new reality, technology like BCIs, AI, and Quantum Computing is not an end in itself but a means to achieve a more responsive, inclusive, and participatory form of governance. The metaverse becomes a digital agora where citizens engage in lively discussions, debates, and decision-making, their voices represented accurately by their digital twins. Policies and welfare programs are no longer static, one-size-fits-all solutions but dynamic responses to the ever-evolving tapestry of societal needs.

**Objectives of the Chapter:**

This chapter aims to explore and present several key aspects of this new reality:

1. **Real-Life Scenarios**: We will delve into various hypothetical scenarios illustrating how MOTMSDD would operate in real-life situations, from urban planning and healthcare to education and environmental policies.

2. **Impact on Governance and Society**: The chapter will examine the broader impacts of MOTMSDD on governance structures, societal dynamics, and the everyday lives of individuals. It will explore how this model fosters a more engaged citizenry and responsive government.

3. **Challenges and Opportunities**: While envisioning the potential of MOTMSDD, the chapter will also address the challenges it presents, including technological feasibility, ethical considerations, and the societal readiness for such a transformation.

4. **The Future of Democracy**: Finally, the chapter will reflect on the implications of MOTMSDD for the future of democracy. It will consider how this model might evolve and adapt, potentially setting the stage for a new era of democratic engagement.

In summary, Section 1 of Chapter 5 introduces readers to the transformative potential of MOTMSDD, setting the groundwork for an in-depth exploration of how this model might reshape our world and redefine the essence of civic engagement and democratic participation.

### Section 2: Real-time Democracy in Action

In this section of "MOTMSDD: The Future of Civic Engagement," we delve into the concept of real-time democracy as envisioned in the MOTMSDD framework and illustrate its application through various hypothetical scenarios.

**Concept of Real-time Democracy:**

Real-time democracy in the context of MOTMSDD is a paradigm shift from traditional democratic practices. Unlike conventional systems where citizen participation is typically limited to periodic voting, real-time democracy under MOTMSDD facilitates continuous and immediate involvement of citizens in governance. This is achieved through the integration of BCIs, AI, and Quantum Computing, allowing for instantaneous collection, analysis, and implementation of public opinion and feedback.

In this model, the decision-making process becomes a dynamic, ongoing dialogue between citizens and their government. Policies and regulations are not just created and then implemented but are continually adapted based on real-time data from the populace. This approach ensures that governance is more responsive, inclusive, and reflective of the current needs and desires of society.

**Hypothetical Scenarios:**

1. **Urban Planning**: Imagine a city facing congestion and pollution challenges. In the MOTMSDD model, urban planners propose several solutions in the metaverse, where each citizen's digital twin can review and provide feedback on these proposals. Data from digital twins, reflecting individual travel patterns, environmental concerns, and lifestyle preferences, are analysed in real-time. This data-driven approach enables the city to implement a hybrid solution combining expanded public transit, new bike lanes, and green spaces, accurately reflecting the diverse needs of its inhabitants.
2. **Healthcare Policy**: In a MOTMSDD world, a healthcare crisis like an emerging pandemic is managed

differently. Real-time health data from citizens' digital twins, along with AI-driven predictive models, allow for quick identification of outbreak hotspots and effective resource allocation. Policies for vaccine distribution or public health measures are dynamically adjusted based on real-time health data and public feedback, ensuring timely and effective responses to the crisis.

3. **Educational Reforms**: In the realm of education, MOTMSDD enables a tailored approach to policy-making. Educational policies are shaped based on direct input from students, parents, and educators via their digital twins. This could lead to the development of diverse educational programs catering to different learning styles, the introduction of new technological tools for education, or the allocation of resources to areas where they are most needed, as indicated by real-time data.

4. **Environmental Policies**: Consider an environmental policy aimed at reducing carbon emissions. In a MOTMSDD-enabled society, citizens contribute their opinions and preferences through their digital twins, influencing the policy directly. Data on citizens' energy consumption patterns, willingness to adopt renewable energy, and feedback on proposed incentives for green initiatives are analysed in real-time, leading to a policy that is both effective in reducing emissions and aligned with public willingness and capability.

In conclusion, Section 2 of Chapter 5 illustrates real-time democracy in action within the MOTMSDD framework, highlighting how it transforms decision-making in various societal aspects. By allowing for continuous and immediate citizen participation, MOTMSDD ensures that governance is agile, adaptive, and truly reflective of the people's will, presenting a new frontier in democratic engagement.

### Section 3: Transforming Governance Structures

In this section of "MOTMSDD: The Future of Civic Engagement," we examine the profound changes that Metaverse Of The Minds Social Direct Democracy (MOTMSDD) could introduce to existing political structures and policy-making processes.

**Changes in Political Structures:**

MOTMSDD has the potential to significantly alter the landscape of political structures, primarily through decentralization and enhanced participatory governance.

1. **Decentralization of Power**: Traditional political systems often centralize decision-making power within a limited group of representatives or governing bodies. MOTMSDD, by contrast, disperses this power among the populace. Through continuous and direct engagement in governance via their digital twins, citizens have a say in decision-making processes that traditionally were the purview of elected officials or bureaucrats.
2. **New Forms of Participatory Governance**: MOTMSDD could lead to the emergence of new governance models that are inherently participatory. This might include digital forums where policy proposals are discussed and refined by citizens in real-time, or platforms where individuals can initiate policy

suggestions directly. Such models promote a more engaged citizenry and ensure that diverse voices are heard in the governance process.

3. **Redefining Representation**: In a MOTMSDD-informed world, the role of elected representatives may evolve. Instead of making decisions on behalf of citizens, representatives might focus on facilitating discussions, ensuring that all segments of the population are represented, and translating the collective will into actionable policies.

## Policy Making in MOTMSDD:

The adoption of MOTMSDD would also bring about significant changes in how policies are formulated and implemented:

1. **Speed and Efficiency**: Thanks to the real-time data processing capabilities of AI and Quantum Computing, policy decisions in a MOTMSDD framework can be made much more rapidly than in traditional systems. This speed does not come at the cost of thoroughness; rather, it is the result of efficient data analysis and the immediate availability of citizen input.

2. **Data-Driven and Inclusive**: Policies in MOTMSDD are formulated based on a wealth of data reflecting the needs, opinions, and preferences of the entire population. This data-driven approach ensures that policies are not only grounded in reality but also inclusive of diverse perspectives.

3. **Dynamic Policy Adaptation**: Unlike the relatively static nature of traditional policy-making, MOTMSDD enables policies to be adaptive. As new data comes in or as

societal needs change, policies can be adjusted in real-time, ensuring they remain relevant and effective.

In conclusion, Section 3 of Chapter 5 outlines the transformative impact that MOTMSDD could have on governance structures. By decentralizing power and enhancing citizen participation, MOTMSDD paves the way for more dynamic, inclusive, and efficient governance. The implementation of this model could signify a significant shift in how political decisions are made and how public policies are crafted and executed, moving towards a more engaged and responsive form of democracy.

### Section 4: Societal Dynamics in a MOTMSDD World
In this section, we explore how the Metaverse Of The Minds Social Direct Democracy (MOTMSDD) model could reshape the landscape of civic engagement, public participation, and the broader social and cultural dynamics.

### Civic Engagement and Public Participation:

The MOTMSDD framework offers a new paradigm for civic engagement and public participation, characterized by increased accessibility and the potential for broader involvement in the democratic process.

1. **Enhanced Accessibility**: With the integration of technologies like BCIs and the metaverse, barriers to participation such as physical disabilities, geographical limitations, and time constraints are significantly reduced. This increased accessibility could lead to

higher levels of civic engagement, as more citizens can conveniently and effectively participate in governance processes.

2. **Digital Literacy and Inclusion**: While MOTMSDD promises greater inclusivity, it also brings the challenge of ensuring digital literacy across all segments of society. Effective implementation of this model requires concerted efforts to enhance digital skills and understanding, ensuring that no group is disenfranchised due to a lack of technological proficiency.

3. **Continuous Engagement**: Unlike traditional democratic systems where citizen involvement is often limited to voting in elections, MOTMSDD allows for continuous participation. Citizens can provide real-time feedback on policies, participate in discussions, and have a direct influence on decision-making processes.

## Social and Cultural Impacts:

The adoption of MOTMSDD would also have profound social and cultural implications.

1. **Shift in Social Norms**: The widespread use of digital twins and participation in a virtual metaverse could lead to changes in social norms and interactions. As people engage more in digital spaces, there could be a shift in how communities are formed and maintained, how social capital is accumulated, and how societal issues are perceived and addressed.

2. **Community Interactions**: MOTMSDD could foster new forms of community interaction and collective action. Digital platforms within the metaverse could become

new public squares, where communities gather not only to discuss governance but also to collaborate on local initiatives, cultural events, and social movements.

3. **Changes in Individual Behaviour**: The continuous feedback loop and the transparency inherent in the MOTMSDD system might encourage more informed and responsible behaviour among citizens. Knowing that their opinions and actions directly impact governance and policy could lead to a more engaged and conscientious citizenry.

4. **Cultural Adaptation**: The integration of diverse cultural perspectives in policy-making, facilitated by MOTMSDD, could lead to a more inclusive and culturally sensitive governance model. This could encourage greater understanding and appreciation of cultural diversity within societies.

In conclusion, Section 4 of Chapter 5 highlights the significant impact that MOTMSDD could have on societal dynamics. By facilitating enhanced civic engagement and reshaping social and cultural interactions, MOTMSDD has the potential to create a more inclusive, participatory, and responsive democratic ecosystem. This model not only redefines the mechanics of democracy but also the very fabric of societal engagement and cultural exchange.

### Section 5: Economic Implications

In this section of "MOTMSDD: The Future of Civic Engagement," we explore the economic implications of a society driven by the Metaverse Of The Minds Social Direct Democracy (MOTMSDD) model, examining how economic systems might adapt and the potential benefits and challenges that could arise.

**Economic Models in MOTMSDD:**

MOTMSDD's integration of advanced technologies and direct democracy could lead to significant changes in economic models and practices:

1. **Resource Allocation**: In a MOTMSDD-driven society, resource allocation could become more efficient and need-based, guided by real-time data from citizens. Economic policies could be dynamically adjusted based on the continuous flow of information about consumption patterns, demographic changes, and citizens' preferences, leading to more responsive and effective resource distribution.
2. **Wealth Distribution**: The focus on individual needs and preferences in MOTMSDD might encourage more equitable economic policies. With a better understanding of the specific needs of different community segments, policies could be tailored to address wealth disparities and provide support where it's most needed, potentially leading to a more balanced distribution of wealth.
3. **New Economic Opportunities**: The widespread use of technologies like BCIs and the metaverse could create new markets and economic opportunities. For example, industries focusing on digital twin technologies, virtual reality, and data analysis could see significant growth.

**Potential Economic Benefits and Challenges:**

The implementation of MOTMSDD could bring various economic benefits and challenges:

1. **Increased Efficiency**: With more data-driven and responsive decision-making, economic policies in a MOTMSDD framework could be more efficient. Reduced bureaucracy and quicker policy adaptation could lead to better economic outcomes and faster responses to market changes.
2. **Job Displacement due to Automation**: While the technological advancements in MOTMSDD could create new jobs, there is also the potential for significant job displacement, particularly in sectors where automation becomes more prevalent. This shift could necessitate new forms of social safety nets and retraining programs for the workforce.
3. **Economic Resilience**: The ability to quickly adapt economic policies based on real-time data could make economies more resilient to shocks, such as financial crises or global events like pandemics. However, this agility requires robust technological infrastructure and a high level of digital literacy across the workforce.
4. **Digital Divide and Economic Inequality**: There is a risk that the benefits of a MOTMSDD-driven economy could be unevenly distributed, exacerbating existing economic inequalities. Ensuring that all segments of society have access to the necessary technology and the skills to participate in this new economy is crucial.

In conclusion, Section 5 of Chapter 5 outlines the potential economic models in a MOTMSDD-driven society and the benefits and challenges that might arise. The transition to such a system promises increased efficiency and potential for more equitable resource distribution, but it also brings challenges like job displacement and the need to address digital divides. As with any significant shift in economic systems, careful planning, inclusive policies, and a focus on education and training will be key to ensuring that the benefits of MOTMSDD are widely and equitably shared.

### Section 6: The Role of Technology and Data

In this section, we delve into the pivotal role of technology and data in the Metaverse Of The Minds Social Direct Democracy (MOTMSDD) model, underscoring how these elements work in tandem to create a responsive and democratic society.

### Technology as a Facilitator:

In the MOTMSDD framework, technology is not just a tool but a facilitator that transforms the very essence of civic engagement and governance.

1. **Brain-Computer Interfaces (BCIs)**: BCIs serve as the direct link between individuals and their digital twins in the metaverse. They allow citizens to communicate their thoughts, opinions, and preferences directly, bypassing traditional forms of interaction. This technology democratizes participation, making it more inclusive and immediate.
2. **Artificial Intelligence (AI)**: AI is the backbone of data analysis in MOTMSDD. It processes the continuous stream of data from millions of digital twins, extracting

actionable insights for policy-making. AI algorithms can identify patterns and trends in public opinion, predict outcomes of policy decisions, and even simulate scenarios to aid in decision-making.

3. **Quantum Computing**: Quantum Computing provides the necessary computational power to manage the vast amounts of data generated within MOTMSDD. Its ability to perform complex calculations at unprecedented speeds is crucial for real-time data processing and analysis, supporting the dynamic and responsive nature of MOTMSDD's decision-making process.

**Data Management and Privacy:**

The effective management of data is a cornerstone of the MOTMSDD model, but it also presents significant challenges in terms of privacy, security, and ethical considerations.

1. **Data Privacy and Security**: With the extensive collection of personal data, safeguarding privacy and ensuring data security are paramount. This involves implementing robust encryption methods, secure data storage solutions, and strict access controls. Clear guidelines and regulations on data usage and privacy must be established and adhered to.

2. **Ethical Data Use**: The ethical implications of using personal data for public policy decision-making cannot be overstated. It is crucial to establish ethical frameworks that guide the use of data, ensuring it is used responsibly and with the consent of the individuals it represents. This includes being transparent about data collection methods, usage purposes, and giving individuals control over their own data.

3. **Managing Data Overload**: The sheer volume of data generated in a MOTMSDD world can lead to challenges in data management. Effective systems for data storage, categorization, and retrieval are essential to prevent data overload and ensure the data's usefulness in decision-making processes.

In conclusion, Section 6 of Chapter 5 emphasizes the fundamental role of technology and data in the MOTMSDD model. While technology facilitates a more inclusive and dynamic form of democracy, managing the data it generates presents challenges that must be addressed through robust privacy protections, ethical frameworks, and efficient data management systems. These components are crucial for maintaining the integrity and trustworthiness of the MOTMSDD model.

### Section 7: Global Perspectives and Adaptation

In the final section of Chapter 5, we explore the global dimensions of the Metaverse Of The Minds Social Direct Democracy (MOTMSDD) model, focusing on how it could be adapted across different countries and cultures and the inherent challenges in achieving global integration.

### Adapting MOTMSDD Globally:

MOTMSDD, with its innovative approach to governance and civic engagement, holds potential for global application, but its implementation would vary significantly based on political, cultural, and technological contexts.

1. **Political Variations**: The adoption of MOTMSDD in different political systems would necessitate customization to align with existing governance structures. In democratic countries, MOTMSDD could enhance existing democratic processes, while in more authoritarian regimes, it might serve as a tool for gradual political liberalization. The degree of decentralization and citizen empowerment would vary based on each country's political landscape.

2. **Cultural Adaptation**: Cultural values and norms play a critical role in shaping governance models. MOTMSDD would need to be adapted to respect and incorporate cultural differences in civic engagement and decision-making. For instance, collective cultures might focus more on community consensus in the MOTMSDD framework, whereas individualistic cultures might emphasize personal choice and autonomy.

3. **Technological Readiness**: The technological infrastructure and digital literacy levels of a country are key factors in implementing MOTMSDD. Developed countries with advanced technological infrastructures and high levels of digital literacy might find it easier to integrate MOTMSDD, while developing countries could face challenges due to limited access to technology and lower digital literacy rates.

**Challenges in Global Integration:**

Integrating MOTMSDD on a global scale poses several challenges and complexities:

1. **Standardization vs. Customization**: Finding the balance between standardizing the core aspects of

MOTMSDD and customizing it to fit local contexts is a major challenge. There needs to be a flexible framework that allows for local adaptation while maintaining the fundamental principles of MOTMSDD.

2. **Addressing the Digital Divide**: A significant challenge in global implementation is the digital divide between countries. Ensuring equitable access to the technologies underpinning MOTMSDD is crucial for its inclusive and democratic nature. This might require international cooperation and investment in digital infrastructure in less developed regions.

3. **Cross-border Data Flow and Privacy**: Implementing MOTMSDD globally would involve the flow of data across borders, which raises concerns about data privacy and security. Establishing international agreements and standards for data protection and privacy would be essential.

4. **Political Resistance and Public Perception**: There may be resistance to adopting MOTMSDD in certain regions due to political apprehension or public scepticism. Overcoming these barriers would require extensive advocacy, education, and demonstration of the model's benefits.

In conclusion, Section 7 of Chapter 5 provides a comprehensive look at the global perspectives and challenges in adapting MOTMSDD. While the potential for positive transformation in governance and civic engagement is immense, realizing this potential on a global scale requires thoughtful consideration of political, cultural, technological, and ethical factors. The successful global integration of MOTMSDD would not only represent a significant advancement in democratic practices but also a testament to the power of technology in bridging diverse communities and fostering a more inclusive and participatory global society.

### *Section 8: Conclusion: A Glimpse into the Future*

As we reach the conclusion of Chapter 5, it is pertinent to reflect on the envisioned impact of Metaverse Of The Minds Social Direct Democracy (MOTMSDD) and to cast our gaze forward to the future that awaits us on this transformative journey.

**Summarizing the Vision:**

MOTMSDD presents a bold reimagining of governance, society, and the economy, leveraging cutting-edge technologies to create a more inclusive, responsive, and dynamic democratic system.

1. **Impact on Governance**: In the MOTMSDD model, governance transcends traditional boundaries, becoming a continuous, interactive process. With the integration of BCIs, AI, and Quantum Computing, decision-making becomes more transparent, participatory, and adaptable to the ever-changing needs and preferences of society.
2. **Transformation of Society**: MOTMSDD envisions a society where civic engagement is not an occasional act but a part of everyday life. This model fosters a sense of community and collective responsibility, encouraging individuals to actively participate in shaping their societal landscape.

3. **Economic Reconfiguration**: Economically, MOTMSDD could lead to more efficient resource allocation, equitable wealth distribution, and the emergence of new markets and job opportunities. It challenges traditional economic models, advocating for an economy that is both dynamic and attuned to the diverse needs of the population.

**Looking Forward:**

As we look towards the future, realizing the vision of MOTMSDD requires ongoing developments and concerted efforts across various domains.

1. **Technological Advancements**: Continued advancements in BCIs, AI, and Quantum Computing are fundamental to the successful implementation of MOTMSDD. These technologies must become more accessible, reliable, and user-friendly to facilitate widespread adoption.
2. **Cultural and Societal Adaptation**: Embracing MOTMSDD requires a cultural shift towards valuing continuous civic engagement and collective decision-making. Educational initiatives and public awareness campaigns will be crucial in preparing societies for this new form of governance.
3. **Policy and Regulatory Frameworks**: Developing supportive policy and regulatory frameworks is essential to ensure that the implementation of MOTMSDD is ethical, secure, and respects individual privacy and rights. International collaboration might be necessary to address the global implications of this model.

4. **Addressing Challenges**: The journey towards a MOTMSDD world will undoubtedly encounter challenges, including ethical dilemmas, privacy concerns, and the risk of digital divides. Addressing these challenges head-on with innovative solutions and robust safeguards will be key to the model's success.

In conclusion, Section 8 of Chapter 5 provides a comprehensive overview of the potential impacts of MOTMSDD and a forward-looking perspective on the journey ahead. The realization of this vision offers a glimpse into a future where technology and democracy converge to create a more engaged, empowered, and equitable world. The journey towards this future will require continued innovation, collaboration, and commitment to shaping a world where every voice is heard and every individual has a stake in the collective well-being of society.

## Chapter 6: Challenges and Considerations

### *Section 1: Introduction to the Challenges*
As we embark on Chapter 6 of "MOTMSDD: The Future of Civic Engagement," it is crucial to acknowledge the complexities and challenges inherent in realizing the vision of Metaverse Of The Minds Social Direct Democracy

(MOTMSDD). This chapter is dedicated to a deep dive into these hurdles, understanding that the path to a transformative societal model is seldom without its obstacles.

**Acknowledging the Hurdles:**

The MOTMSDD concept, while revolutionary and promising, confronts a myriad of challenges that span technological, ethical, social, and political domains.

1. **Technological Barriers**: The technological foundation of MOTMSDD – comprising BCIs, AI, and Quantum Computing – is still evolving. Ensuring these technologies are reliable, accessible, and user-friendly for widespread adoption poses significant challenges. There are also concerns about data security, system integrity, and the robustness of the infrastructure required to support such an intricate system.
2. **Ethical and Privacy Concerns**: The extensive collection and analysis of personal data in MOTMSDD raise substantial ethical questions and privacy concerns. Balancing the benefits of data-driven decision-making with the need to protect individual privacy and prevent misuse of information is a significant challenge.
3. **Cultural and Social Acceptance**: MOTMSDD proposes a drastic shift in how individuals engage with governance and each other. Achieving broad cultural and social acceptance of this new model requires overcoming skepticism, addressing fears of technological dominance, and ensuring inclusivity in a diverse societal landscape.
4. **Political and Regulatory Hurdles**: Integrating MOTMSDD within existing political frameworks and

ensuring regulatory compliance is another challenge. This involves navigating complex legal landscapes, adapting to different governance structures, and potentially influencing policy to accommodate this new model of democracy.

**Scope of the Chapter:**

This chapter will methodically explore these challenges, understanding their intricacies, and proposing pathways to address them. The following will be covered:

1. **In-depth Analysis of Technological Challenges**: A closer look at the technological advancements needed, the infrastructural requirements, and the strategies to ensure system reliability and security.
2. **Ethical and Privacy Considerations**: An exploration of the ethical dilemmas posed by MOTMSDD, strategies for safeguarding privacy, and frameworks for ethical data use.
3. **Cultural and Social Integration**: Discussion on strategies to foster societal acceptance, cultural adaptability, and inclusive engagement within the MOTMSDD framework.
4. **Navigating Political and Regulatory Landscapes**: Examination of the political implications of implementing MOTMSDD and the necessary regulatory adjustments to facilitate its integration.

In conclusion, Section 1 of Chapter 6 sets the stage for a comprehensive exploration of the challenges in realizing the MOTMSDD vision. Acknowledging and addressing these challenges is not just a hurdle to overcome; it is a crucial step in ensuring the successful, ethical, and sustainable implementation of this groundbreaking model of civic engagement.

### *Section 2: Ethical Considerations*

In this critical section of "MOTMSDD: The Future of Civic Engagement," we delve into the ethical complexities surrounding the technologies and concepts central to Metaverse Of The Minds Social Direct Democracy (MOTMSDD), particularly focusing on brain-computer interfaces (BCI), artificial intelligence (AI), and the balance between individual rights and collective interests.

### The Ethics of BCI and AI:

The integration of BCI and AI in MOTMSDD brings to the fore a range of ethical issues that require careful consideration:

1. **Consent and Autonomy**: The use of BCIs raises questions about consent and personal autonomy. How do we ensure that individuals are fully aware and consenting to the extent of their neural data being accessed and used? It is essential to establish clear consent protocols and to ensure that individuals retain autonomy over their thoughts and decisions, without undue influence from the technology.
2. **Potential for Manipulation**: There is an inherent risk of manipulation with AI algorithms interpreting neural data and potentially influencing decision-making. Safeguards must be in place to prevent manipulation

and to ensure that AI algorithms are transparent and unbiased.

3. **Mental Privacy**: BCIs have the potential to access thoughts and subconscious processes. Protecting mental privacy becomes paramount, and ethical guidelines must be established to define the boundaries of what is permissible in terms of data collection and analysis.

**Balancing Individual Rights and Collective Interest:**

The MOTMSDD model presents unique challenges in balancing individual rights with the collective interest, a fundamental ethical dilemma:

1. **Data Usage for Public Policy**: While the use of individual data can significantly enhance public policy-making, it must be balanced against the right to privacy. Establishing guidelines on how much data can be used, in what ways, and with what limitations is crucial.

2. **Equity and Fairness**: Ensuring that MOTMSDD does not exacerbate existing inequalities is vital. This includes careful consideration of how decisions are made and whose voices are heard, ensuring that minority views are not overshadowed by the majority.

**Diverse Ethical Perspectives:**

MOTMSDD, being a globally applicable model, must consider the diversity of ethical perspectives across different cultures and societies:

1. **Cultural Variations in Ethical Norms**: Different cultures have varying perspectives on privacy, autonomy, and collective responsibility. The ethical framework of MOTMSDD must be adaptable to these variations, respecting cultural norms and values.
2. **Global Ethical Standards**: While adapting to local contexts, there needs to be a set of global ethical standards that guide the core operation of MOTMSDD. This includes universal principles on human rights, data protection, and transparency.

In conclusion, Section 2 of Chapter 6 addresses the profound ethical considerations intrinsic to the implementation of MOTMSDD. Tackling these ethical challenges head-on is essential for the legitimacy and success of the MOTMSDD model. It requires a multifaceted approach, combining technological safeguards with robust ethical frameworks, ensuring that the revolutionary potential of MOTMSDD is realized in a manner that is respectful of individual rights and sensitive to diverse cultural contexts.

### Section 3: Privacy Concerns

In Section 3 of "MOTMSDD: The Future of Civic Engagement," we address the crucial issue of privacy in the context of the Metaverse Of The Minds Social Direct Democracy (MOTMSDD) model. This section explores the intricacies of data privacy in the digital age, specifically focusing on how MOTMSDD handles personal data and the challenges posed by varying global privacy standards.

**Data Privacy in the Digital Age:**

In a world increasingly driven by data, privacy concerns have escalated, particularly with technologies that continuously collect and analyse personal information.

1. **The Value of Privacy**: Privacy is not just a personal preference but a fundamental human right. In the digital age, where data is a valuable asset, ensuring the privacy of individuals' data is critical. This includes protecting against unauthorized access, misuse, and potential exploitation of personal information.
2. **Risks of Data Breaches**: With vast amounts of data being collected, the risk of data breaches increases. These breaches can lead to sensitive information falling into the wrong hands, which can have serious repercussions for individuals' privacy and security.

**MOTMSDD's Data Handling:**

The MOTMSDD model, which relies heavily on personal data from digital twins and BCIs, faces significant challenges in ensuring privacy.

1. **Safeguarding Personal Data**: MOTMSDD needs to implement robust data protection measures. This includes secure encryption of data, strict access controls, and regular audits to ensure data security.
2. **Consent and Transparency**: It is imperative for MOTMSDD to have clear protocols regarding consent for data collection and usage. Users should be fully informed about what data is being collected, how it is being used, and who has access to it.
3. **Anonymization and Data Minimization**: Whenever possible, MOTMSDD should employ data

anonymization techniques to prevent the identification of individuals. Additionally, data minimization principles should be adhered to, ensuring that only necessary data is collected.

**Global Privacy Standards:**

Implementing MOTMSDD in different global contexts presents additional challenges due to varying privacy standards and regulations.

1. **Navigating Diverse Regulations**: Different countries have different laws and regulations regarding data privacy (like the GDPR in the European Union). MOTMSDD must be adaptable to comply with these varying regulations while maintaining its core functionality.
2. **Harmonizing Standards**: One of the significant challenges for MOTMSDD is to find a way to harmonize its operations across these different legal landscapes. This may involve developing a flexible framework that can be customized to meet regional privacy requirements.
3. **International Cooperation**: Effective implementation of MOTMSDD on a global scale may require international cooperation to create standards and guidelines that respect data privacy while allowing for the seamless operation of the model across borders.

In conclusion, Section 3 of Chapter 6 underscores the importance of addressing privacy concerns in the implementation of MOTMSDD. Ensuring data privacy is not just about technical solutions; it is about building trust, respecting individual rights, and creating a sustainable model that aligns with global standards and regulations. As MOTMSDD moves forward, navigating these privacy challenges will be crucial to its success and acceptance.

### *Section 4: Addressing the Digital Divide*

In Section 4 of "MOTMSDD: The Future of Civic Engagement," we delve into the critical issue of the digital divide, exploring its definition, implications for the implementation of MOTMSDD, and strategies for bridging this gap to ensure equitable participation.

### Defining the Digital Divide:

The digital divide refers to the disparities between individuals, communities, and regions in terms of access to information and communication technologies, including the internet, digital devices, and digital literacy skills. This divide can significantly impact the ability of people to participate in digital platforms, such as those proposed in MOTMSDD, leading to unequal opportunities and benefits.

1. **Access to Technology**: One aspect of the digital divide is the disparity in access to technology. This includes not only physical devices but also internet connectivity. In many parts of the world, especially in less developed regions, access to reliable internet and modern digital devices is limited.
2. **Digital Literacy**: Another crucial aspect is digital literacy, which involves the skills needed to effectively use digital technologies. A lack of digital literacy can

prevent individuals from fully participating in digital platforms and online decision-making processes.

**Bridging the Gap:**

For MOTMSDD to be truly inclusive and effective, it is essential to address these disparities.

1. **Infrastructure Development**: Investing in digital infrastructure is key to reducing the technology access gap. This includes expanding internet connectivity, especially in rural and underserved areas, and providing affordable digital devices.
2. **Education and Training**: Equipping individuals with digital literacy skills is vital. Educational initiatives should focus on imparting digital skills across all age groups and communities, ensuring that everyone can navigate and participate in the MOTMSDD model.
3. **Subsidies and Incentives**: Governments and organizations could offer subsidies or incentives for technology access to low-income groups or marginalized communities, helping to level the playing field.

**Equitable Participation in MOTMSDD:**

Ensuring that MOTMSDD is equitable involves more than just providing access; it also means actively engaging underrepresented groups.

1. **Targeted Outreach**: Efforts should be made to reach out to marginalized communities and involve them in the development and implementation of MOTMSDD.

This can help ensure that the system is designed with their needs and circumstances in mind.

2. **Diverse Representation**: It's crucial to have diverse representation in the planning and decision-making stages of MOTMSDD. This diversity helps in understanding and addressing the unique challenges faced by different communities.

3. **Accessible Design**: The MOTMSDD platform should be designed with accessibility in mind, ensuring that it is user-friendly for people with varying levels of technological expertise and for those with disabilities.

In conclusion, Section 4 of Chapter 6 highlights the importance of addressing the digital divide in the implementation of MOTMSDD. Overcoming this divide is crucial to ensuring that MOTMSDD is a truly inclusive, democratic, and effective model of civic engagement. By investing in infrastructure, education, and targeted outreach, MOTMSDD can bridge the gap in digital access and literacy, paving the way for equitable participation from all segments of society.

### Section 5: Implementation Challenges

In Section 5 of "MOTMSDD: The Future of Civic Engagement," we explore the multifaceted challenges associated with implementing the Metaverse Of The Minds Social Direct Democracy (MOTMSDD) model. This section addresses technological barriers, infrastructural needs, resource allocation, and the hurdles in scaling up the model from a conceptual framework to a widespread reality.

**Technological Barriers:**

Implementing MOTMSDD requires advanced technologies that are still in developmental stages, presenting several barriers.

1. **Limitations in Current BCI Technology**: While Brain-Computer Interface (BCI) technology has made significant strides, it still faces limitations in terms of accuracy, user-friendliness, and non-invasiveness. Developing BCIs that can seamlessly and accurately interpret a wide range of neural signals in a user-friendly manner is a significant challenge.
2. **AI Technology and Ethical Algorithms**: Artificial Intelligence (AI) is a cornerstone of MOTMSDD, but developing AI systems that are ethical, unbiased, and transparent is a major technological and ethical challenge. Ensuring that AI algorithms can handle the complexity and diversity of human data without inherent biases is crucial.
3. **Quantum Computing Infrastructure**: Although Quantum Computing holds immense potential for data processing and analysis, its practical application is still emerging. Building the necessary quantum computing infrastructure to support the vast data requirements of MOTMSDD is a formidable task.

**Infrastructure and Resource Allocation:**

The establishment of a MOTMSDD framework demands significant infrastructural development and resource allocation.

1. **Building Digital Infrastructure**: A robust digital infrastructure, including high-speed internet connectivity and data centres, is essential for the MOTMSDD model. Ensuring this infrastructure is uniformly accessible across different regions poses a substantial challenge, especially in less developed areas.
2. **Resource Allocation for Development and Maintenance**: Allocating sufficient resources for the development, deployment, and maintenance of the MOTMSDD infrastructure is crucial. This includes financial investment, human resources for development and operations, and ongoing support for system updates and security.

**Scaling Up:**

Taking MOTMSDD from a theoretical model to widespread implementation involves several scaling challenges.

1. **From Pilot Projects to Broad Adoption**: Initial pilot projects need to be carefully designed to test the MOTMSDD model in controlled environments. Learning from these pilots and scaling the model to broader applications require strategic planning, substantial investment, and incremental implementation.
2. **Public Acceptance and Participation**: Gaining public acceptance and encouraging active participation are key to scaling up MOTMSDD. This involves public education campaigns, demonstrations of the system's benefits, and addressing public concerns about privacy and technology use.
3. **International Collaboration**: Given the global nature of the MOTMSDD model, international collaboration is

necessary for its scaling. This includes harmonizing standards, ensuring interoperability of systems across borders, and navigating diverse regulatory environments.

In conclusion, Section 5 of Chapter 6 delves into the significant challenges in implementing the MOTMSDD model. Overcoming these hurdles requires not only technological advancements but also strategic planning, resource allocation, public engagement, and international cooperation. Successfully addressing these implementation challenges is key to realizing the vision of MOTMSDD as a transformative tool for democratic engagement and governance.

## *Section 6: Legal and Regulatory Hurdles*

Section 6 of "MOTMSDD: The Future of Civic Engagement" addresses the legal and regulatory challenges involved in integrating the Metaverse Of The Minds Social Direct Democracy (MOTMSDD) into existing governance structures and the necessity for developing new regulations to support this innovative model.

**Navigating Legal Frameworks:**

Integrating MOTMSDD within the existing legal landscape presents several complex challenges:

1. **Compatibility with Existing Laws**: One of the primary challenges is ensuring that MOTMSDD aligns with current legal frameworks. This includes laws related to data privacy, telecommunications, cyber security, and

human rights. The model must operate within these legal confines while striving to achieve its objective of enhanced civic engagement.

2. **Jurisdictional Issues**: Given the global nature of the internet and the digital realm, MOTMSDD faces the challenge of navigating different legal jurisdictions. This is particularly complex when considering cross-border data flows and the varying legal standards and protections in different countries.

3. **Legal Status of Digital Twins**: The concept of digital twins in MOTMSDD raises unique legal questions. Determining the legal status of these digital entities, their rights, and how they interact with the law is an uncharted territory that requires careful legal consideration.

**Developing New Regulations:**

The implementation of MOTMSDD also necessitates the development of new regulations and legal frameworks to support its operation.

1. **Regulating New Technologies**: The cutting-edge technologies central to MOTMSDD, such as BCIs and quantum computing, currently operate in a largely unregulated space. There is a need for new regulations that address the ethical use, safety standards, and quality control of these technologies.

2. **Data Governance Laws**: Given the heavy reliance on data in MOTMSDD, there is a critical need for robust data governance laws. These laws should address data collection, storage, processing, and sharing practices, ensuring they are done ethically and responsibly.

3. **Protecting Citizens' Rights**: New legal frameworks must ensure that citizens' rights are protected in the digital realm, particularly concerning privacy, consent, and freedom of expression. These frameworks should be flexible enough to adapt to technological advancements while maintaining strong protections for individual rights.

4. **International Standards and Cooperation**: The global nature of MOTMSDD necessitates international cooperation in developing legal standards and frameworks. This includes harmonizing regulations across borders and establishing international guidelines for data privacy, cyber security, and technology use.

In conclusion, Section 6 of Chapter 6 highlights the legal and regulatory hurdles that must be navigated to successfully integrate MOTMSDD into existing governance systems and the necessity for new legal frameworks that can accommodate this innovative model. Addressing these legal and regulatory challenges is crucial for the practical and ethical implementation of MOTMSDD, ensuring that it operates within a safe, secure, and legally compliant environment.

### Section 7: Societal Readiness and Acceptance
In Section 7 of "MOTMSDD: The Future of Civic Engagement," we address the crucial aspects of societal readiness and acceptance, which are pivotal for the successful implementation of the Metaverse Of The Minds Social Direct Democracy (MOTMSDD) model.

**Public Perception and Trust:**

The success of MOTMSDD is heavily reliant on how it is perceived by the public and the level of trust it garners.

1. **Building Trust in New Technology**: Introducing advanced technologies like BCIs, AI, and Quantum Computing in governance requires building public trust. This involves demonstrating the safety, reliability, and benefits of these technologies, along with transparent communication about their use and implications.
2. **Addressing Privacy Concerns**: Given the extensive data collection involved in MOTMSDD, addressing privacy concerns is critical for building trust. The public needs assurance that their personal data is secure and that privacy is respected.
3. **Myths and Misinformation**: Combatting myths and misinformation about MOTMSDD is essential. Public education campaigns can help in clarifying misconceptions and providing accurate information about the model's functionality and benefits.

**Cultural and Social Adaptation:**

Adopting MOTMSDD involves significant cultural and social adaptation to a new model of governance and societal interaction.

1. **Shift in Governance Participation**: MOTMSDD proposes a shift from traditional representative governance to a more participatory model. This shift requires a cultural change in how individuals view their

role in governance and their willingness to engage actively.

2. **Adaptation to Digital Interaction**: The emphasis on digital interaction in MOTMSDD might be a significant shift for many, especially for communities with limited digital engagement. Encouraging and facilitating this adaptation is vital for inclusive participation.

3. **Diversity and Inclusivity**: Ensuring that MOTMSDD is adaptable to diverse cultural contexts and inclusive of various social groups is crucial. This involves understanding and integrating different cultural perspectives and addressing any barriers to participation that might exist for marginalized groups.

4. **Social Norms and Values**: As MOTMSDD integrates into society, it may influence and be influenced by existing social norms and values. Navigating these dynamics respectfully and thoughtfully is essential for the harmonious integration of the model into different societal contexts.

In conclusion, Section 7 of Chapter 6 delves into the complex dynamics of societal readiness and acceptance for the MOTMSDD model. Building public trust, ensuring cultural and social adaptation, and addressing privacy and misinformation concerns are key for the successful implementation of MOTMSDD. This section underscores the importance of considering and actively working on these aspects to foster an environment where MOTMSDD can be effectively and seamlessly integrated into the societal fabric.

*Section 8: Conclusion: Overcoming the Hurdles*

As we conclude Chapter 6 of "MOTMSDD: The Future of Civic Engagement," it is imperative to reflect on the key challenges outlined and consider the path forward in overcoming these hurdles to realize the potential of Metaverse Of The Minds Social Direct Democracy (MOTMSDD).

**Summarizing Key Challenges:**

Throughout this chapter, we have delved into various significant challenges that stand in the way of implementing MOTMSDD:

1. **Ethical Considerations**: The ethical implications of using technologies like BCIs and AI pose complex questions about consent, autonomy, and the ethical use of data.
2. **Privacy Concerns**: Ensuring the privacy and security of the vast amounts of personal data that MOTMSDD relies on is a paramount concern, with the need for robust data protection measures.
3. **Implementation Hurdles**: The technological barriers, infrastructural needs, and the challenges in scaling up MOTMSDD from concept to reality present significant obstacles.
4. **Legal and Regulatory Issues**: Navigating the existing legal frameworks and developing new regulations to support the innovative MOTMSDD model requires careful consideration and adaptation.

5. **Societal Readiness and Acceptance**: Building public trust, ensuring cultural and social adaptation, and addressing privacy concerns are crucial for the model's acceptance and success.

**Path Forward:**

Despite these challenges, the path forward towards realizing MOTMSDD is paved with opportunity and potential for transformative change:

1. **Collaborative Solutions**: Addressing these challenges requires a collaborative approach, involving experts from various fields, including technology, law, ethics, and social sciences. Cross-disciplinary dialogue and partnerships are key to developing holistic solutions.
2. **Technological Advancements and Research**: Continued research and development in the fields of BCIs, AI, and Quantum Computing are essential. This involves not only technological advancements but also research into their societal impacts and ethical implications.
3. **Public Engagement and Education**: Actively engaging with the public, educating them about the benefits and implications of MOTMSDD, and addressing their concerns is crucial for gaining trust and acceptance.
4. **Policy Development and International Cooperation**: Developing supportive policies and engaging in international cooperation will be vital in navigating legal and regulatory challenges. This includes setting global standards and working towards harmonized legal frameworks.

5. **Incremental Implementation and Pilot Projects**: Implementing MOTMSDD in phases, starting with pilot projects, can provide valuable insights and data to guide the model's broader application. These pilots can serve as testbeds for refining the system and addressing practical challenges.

In conclusion, Section 8 of Chapter 6 emphasizes that while the journey towards implementing MOTMSDD is fraught with challenges, these obstacles are not insurmountable. Through collaborative efforts, continuous innovation, public engagement, and careful policy development, the hurdles can be overcome. The path forward involves a commitment to ongoing dialogue and development, ensuring that the MOTMSDD model evolves in a manner that is ethically sound, technologically feasible, legally compliant, and socially accepted. The vision of MOTMSDD represents a significant step forward in the evolution of civic engagement and democracy, promising a future where technology enhances democratic participation and governance in unprecedented ways.

---

## Chapter 7: Preparing for a MOTMSDD Future

*Section 1: Introduction to the Road Ahead*
As we begin Chapter 7 of "MOTMSDD: The Future of Civic Engagement," we set the context for the transformative journey towards realizing the Metaverse Of The Minds Social Direct Democracy (MOTMSDD) vision. This chapter aims to provide a comprehensive roadmap, highlighting the preparation and adaptation required for transitioning to a future shaped by MOTMSDD.

## Setting the Context:

MOTMSDD represents a paradigm shift in how we perceive and engage with democratic processes and governance. Its implementation carries the potential to radically transform the landscape of civic engagement, making it more inclusive, responsive, and efficient. However, such transformation does not come without its challenges.

1. **The Transformative Potential**: At its core, MOTMSDD offers a vision where technology and democracy intertwine to enhance participation and representation. This model proposes a future where every individual's voice is heard and valued through continuous, direct engagement facilitated by cutting-edge technologies like BCIs, AI, and Quantum Computing.
2. **Need for Preparation and Adaptation**: Embracing this futuristic model requires significant preparation and adaptation at various levels – technological, legal, ethical, societal, and cultural. It involves not only the development and refinement of technologies but also

the creation of supportive infrastructures, policies, and social norms that foster and sustain this new model of governance.

**Objectives of the Chapter:**

This chapter is dedicated to charting a path forward, outlining key steps and strategies necessary for transitioning to a MOTMSDD-driven society.

1. **Technological Advancements**: Discussing the ongoing advancements in technology that are essential for the practical implementation of MOTMSDD, including improvements in BCI technology, AI algorithms, and Quantum Computing capabilities.
2. **Policy and Legal Frameworks**: Addressing the need for developing robust policy and legal frameworks that can support the MOTMSDD model, ensuring it operates within ethical boundaries and respects individual rights.
3. **Cultural and Societal Shifts**: Exploring the cultural and societal shifts required for MOTMSDD to be successfully integrated into daily life, including promoting digital literacy, fostering a culture of active civic participation, and addressing potential resistance to change.
4. **Global Cooperation and Standards**: Highlighting the importance of international cooperation and the establishment of global standards and best practices for data privacy, security, and technology use in the context of MOTMSDD.

In conclusion, Section 1 of Chapter 7 sets the stage for a deep dive into the roadmap for a MOTMSDD future. It underscores the importance of comprehensive preparation and adaptation across multiple domains to ensure the successful realization of this visionary model. The journey ahead is complex and multi-faceted, but with careful planning and collaborative effort, the MOTMSDD vision can be transformed into a reality, marking a new era in the evolution of democracy and civic engagement.

- 

### *Section 2: Building the Technological Foundation*

In Section 2 of "MOTMSDD: The Future of Civic Engagement," we delve into the crucial aspect of developing the technological foundation necessary for the Metaverse Of The Minds Social Direct Democracy (MOTMSDD). This section focuses on the advancements and infrastructural development required to make MOTMSDD a viable and effective model of governance and civic participation.

**Developing Necessary Technologies:**

The successful implementation of MOTMSDD hinges on the development and refinement of several key technologies:

1. **Advancements in Brain-Computer Interfaces (BCIs)**: For MOTMSDD to function optimally, BCIs need to be advanced in terms of accuracy, user-friendliness, and non-invasive methods. Research and development efforts should focus on creating BCIs that can seamlessly and efficiently interpret a wide range of neural signals, allowing for intuitive and accessible interaction between users and the MOTMSDD platform.
2. **Artificial Intelligence (AI) Development**: AI is integral to processing and analysing the vast data generated

within the MOTMSDD framework. Continuous improvement in AI algorithms is necessary for handling complex data sets, ensuring ethical decision-making, and providing unbiased analysis. This includes developing AI systems that are transparent, explainable, and respectful of privacy norms.

3. **Quantum Computing Advancements**: Quantum computing has the potential to process information at unprecedented speeds, making it essential for managing the data needs of MOTMSDD. Advancing quantum computing technology will involve enhancing computational power, ensuring system stability, and making it more accessible for practical applications.

**Infrastructure Development:**

The establishment of MOTMSDD also demands significant infrastructural groundwork:

1. **Digital Network Expansion**: A robust and widespread digital network is the backbone of MOTMSDD. This involves not only expanding internet connectivity, especially in underserved areas, but also ensuring the reliability and speed of these networks to support real-time data processing and interaction within the MOTMSDD ecosystem.

2. **Data Centre Infrastructure**: Developing data centres equipped to handle the storage and processing needs of MOTMSDD is crucial. These centres must be secure, efficient, and capable of managing large volumes of data with minimal latency. Additionally, considering the global nature of MOTMSDD, data centres need to be

strategically located to ensure efficient data flow across different regions.

3. **Security and Data Protection**: As MOTMSDD will handle sensitive personal data, the infrastructure must be designed with stringent security measures. This includes advanced cybersecurity protocols, regular security audits, and the incorporation of fail-safe mechanisms to protect against data breaches and cyber-attacks.

In conclusion, Section 2 of Chapter 7 outlines the necessary steps for building the technological foundation of MOTMSDD. It highlights the importance of advancing BCIs, AI, and quantum computing, and establishing robust digital infrastructure to support the operational needs of MOTMSDD. This technological groundwork is not just about creating new systems; it's about ensuring that these systems are reliable, ethical, secure, and accessible to all, forming the backbone of a future where MOTMSDD can thrive as a new paradigm of civic engagement and governance.

### *Section 3: Policy Frameworks and Governance*
In Section 3 of "MOTMSDD: The Future of Civic Engagement," we turn our attention to the essential aspects of policy frameworks and governance that need to be developed to facilitate the successful implementation and integration of the Metaverse Of The Minds Social Direct Democracy (MOTMSDD).

**Creating Supportive Policies:**

The establishment of MOTMSDD requires a foundational shift in existing policies and the creation of new governance models that can accommodate its innovative approach:

1. **Inclusive Policy Development**: Policies need to be formulated to ensure that the MOTMSDD framework is inclusive and accessible to all segments of society. This includes creating policies that address the digital divide, promote digital literacy, and ensure equitable access to the technology required for MOTMSDD.
2. **Data Governance and Privacy Policies**: Given the central role of data in MOTMSDD, robust data governance policies are crucial. These should encompass data privacy, consent mechanisms, data storage and security protocols, and ethical guidelines for data usage.
3. **Participatory Governance Models**: MOTMSDD advocates for a more participatory form of governance. Policies need to be designed to support this model, enabling continuous and effective citizen engagement in decision-making processes. This includes establishing frameworks for digital participation, ensuring transparency, and creating mechanisms for feedback and accountability.

**Regulatory Considerations:**

Implementing MOTMSDD also requires careful consideration of new regulations and legal frameworks:

1. **Adapting Legal Frameworks for Emerging Technologies**: The legal implications of technologies like BCIs, AI, and Quantum Computing need to be

thoroughly understood and addressed. This involves updating existing laws or creating new regulations to cover issues such as intellectual property rights, liability in the use of AI, and ethical standards for BCIs.

2. **Cross-Jurisdictional Regulatory Challenges**: Since MOTMSDD has the potential to operate across borders, harmonizing regulations across different jurisdictions becomes crucial. This includes ensuring compliance with international data protection laws, cyber security standards, and technology use policies.

3. **Regulations for Digital Twins and Virtual Spaces**: The concept of digital twins and virtual spaces within the MOTMSDD model presents unique regulatory challenges. Laws need to be developed or adapted to govern the rights and responsibilities associated with digital twins, as well as the management and oversight of virtual spaces used for civic engagement.

4. **Continuous Regulatory Evolution**: Given the rapid pace of technological advancement, regulatory frameworks for MOTMSDD must be flexible and adaptable. This requires a proactive approach to regulation, with continuous monitoring and updating of laws and policies to keep pace with technological and societal changes.

In conclusion, Section 3 of Chapter 7 highlights the importance of developing supportive policy frameworks and robust governance models to facilitate the transition to a MOTMSDD future. These frameworks and models must be comprehensive, inclusive, and adaptable, ensuring that they provide a solid foundation for the innovative and participatory nature of MOTMSDD while addressing the challenges posed by emerging technologies and the digital transformation of governance.

### Section 4: The Role of Education and Awareness

In Section 4 of "MOTMSDD: The Future of Civic Engagement," we address the pivotal role of education and awareness in facilitating the transition to the Metaverse Of The Minds Social Direct Democracy (MOTMSDD) model. This section focuses on the strategies for educating the public and developing necessary skills for engaging with the MOTMSDD system.

### Educating the Public:

Public understanding and support are essential for the successful adoption of MOTMSDD.

1. **Awareness Campaigns**: Comprehensive awareness campaigns are needed to introduce the public to the concept of MOTMSDD. These campaigns should explain the model's fundamentals, how it differs from traditional forms of governance, and its potential to enhance democratic participation. Using various media channels, including social media, television, and community events, can help reach a broad audience.
2. **Highlighting Benefits and Addressing Concerns**: It's crucial to communicate the benefits of MOTMSDD, such as increased civic engagement, real-time decision-making, and personalized representation. Simultaneously, potential concerns and challenges should be addressed transparently, including issues of privacy, technology reliance, and data security. This

balanced approach will help in building trust and support for the model.

3. **Public Dialogues and Forums**: Encouraging public dialogues and forums where citizens can ask questions, express concerns, and provide feedback about MOTMSDD is important. These platforms can be instrumental in understanding public sentiment and making necessary adjustments to the model.

## Training and Skill Development:

For MOTMSDD to be effective, citizens need to have the skills to interact with this new system.

1. **Digital Literacy Programs**: Implementing digital literacy programs is essential, especially in communities with low levels of digital engagement. These programs should cover basic digital skills, including how to access and navigate the MOTMSDD platform, ensuring that everyone, regardless of their background, can participate.

2. **Specialized Training for Various Stakeholders**: Different stakeholders in the MOTMSDD model, such as administrators, policy makers, and technical support staff, will require specialized training. For administrators and policy makers, understanding how to interpret and use data from the MOTMSDD system is crucial. Technical staff will need training in maintaining and troubleshooting the system.

3. **Educational Curriculum Integration**: Integrating concepts related to MOTMSDD, civic technology, and digital democracy into educational curricula can prepare future generations for active participation in

this model. This could include modules in schools and universities that focus on digital citizenship, data ethics, and civic technology.

In conclusion, Section 4 of Chapter 7 emphasizes the importance of education and awareness in the journey towards a MOTMSDD future. By educating the public, addressing their concerns, and equipping them with the necessary skills, the transition to MOTMSDD can be smooth and inclusive, ensuring that all segments of society are prepared and empowered to engage in this innovative model of governance and civic participation.

### Section 5: Involving Individuals and Communities

Section 5 of "MOTMSDD: The Future of Civic Engagement" focuses on the crucial role of individual and community involvement in the successful implementation and evolution of the Metaverse Of The Minds Social Direct Democracy (MOTMSDD). This section explores strategies for engaging communities and encouraging individual contributions to shape and adopt the MOTMSDD model effectively.

**Community Engagement:**

The active participation of communities is key to the practical realization of MOTMSDD.

1. **Grassroots Involvement**: Encouraging grassroots involvement in the development and implementation of MOTMSDD is crucial. This can be achieved through community meetings, workshops, and forums where

residents can learn about MOTMSDD, voice their opinions, and offer suggestions. Engaging communities in this way helps ensure that the system reflects the diverse needs and preferences of its users.

2. **Community Pilot Programs**: Implementing community-based pilot programs is an effective way to test and refine the MOTMSDD model. These pilots can provide valuable insights into how the system works in real-world settings, allowing for adjustments and improvements based on community feedback.

3. **Local Leaders and Influencers**: Involving local leaders and influencers in promoting and educating about MOTMSDD can enhance community engagement. These individuals can act as ambassadors for the model, helping to build trust and acceptance within their communities.

**Individual Contributions:**

Every individual has the potential to contribute to the development and success of MOTMSDD.

1. **Participation in Pilot Projects**: Individuals can participate in pilot projects or trials of the MOTMSDD system. Their experiences and feedback are invaluable in identifying strengths and areas for improvement. This direct involvement also fosters a sense of ownership and investment in the model's success.

2. **Feedback Mechanisms**: Establishing robust feedback mechanisms is essential to capture individuals' insights and experiences with MOTMSDD. This can include digital platforms for feedback, surveys, and suggestion boxes. Regularly reviewing and acting on this feedback

ensures that the system remains responsive to the users' needs.

3. **Volunteering and Advocacy**: Encouraging individuals to volunteer in MOTMSDD-related activities or advocacy can further enhance community engagement. Volunteers can help in educating others about the system, assisting in data collection, or participating in community outreach programs.

4. **Social Media and Online Communities**: Leveraging social media and online communities can be a powerful tool for involving individuals. These platforms can be used for information dissemination, discussion forums, and gathering community input. They also provide a space for individuals to connect, share experiences, and collaborate on MOTMSDD-related initiatives.

In conclusion, Section 5 of Chapter 7 underscores the importance of actively involving individuals and communities in the development, testing, and refinement of the MOTMSDD model. Through community engagement and individual contributions, MOTMSDD can be shaped into a system that truly reflects and serves the diverse needs of its users, ensuring its relevance, effectiveness, and acceptance in society. The collective effort of communities and individuals is integral to the successful realization of the MOTMSDD vision, marking a new chapter in participatory governance and civic engagement.

### *Section 6: Fostering Collaboration and Innovation*
In Section 6 of "MOTMSDD: The Future of Civic Engagement," the focus is on the pivotal role of collaboration and innovation

in the development and realization of the Metaverse Of The Minds Social Direct Democracy (MOTMSDD). This section explores the necessity for cross-sector collaboration and the creation of innovation ecosystems to support the growth and effectiveness of MOTMSDD.

**Cross-Sector Collaboration:**

The successful implementation of MOTMSDD requires a synergistic collaboration across various sectors:

1. **Government and Policy Makers**: Governments play a crucial role in providing the regulatory framework and support necessary for MOTMSDD. They can facilitate public-private partnerships, provide funding for research, and create policies that encourage the development and adoption of MOTMSDD technologies.
2. **Private Sector Involvement**: The expertise and resources of the private sector are invaluable in the technological development of MOTMSDD. Collaborating with tech companies, startups, and industry leaders can lead to innovative solutions and advancements in BCIs, AI, and Quantum Computing.
3. **Academic and Research Institutions**: Academia contributes through research and development, particularly in addressing the theoretical and practical challenges of MOTMSDD. Universities and research institutions can conduct studies, pilot projects, and experiments to test and refine the model.
4. **Civil Society and NGOs**: Civil society organizations and NGOs can provide insights into community needs, help in advocating the model, and facilitate public engagement and education. Their involvement ensures

that MOTMSDD remains aligned with societal values and public interests.

**Innovation Ecosystems:**

Creating ecosystems that nurture innovation is essential for the continuous development and improvement of MOTMSDD.

1. **Research and Development Hubs**: Establishing dedicated R&D hubs for MOTMSDD can accelerate innovation. These hubs can serve as centres for experimentation, bringing together experts from various fields to collaborate on technological and societal aspects of MOTMSDD.
2. **Funding for Innovation**: Securing funding is critical for fostering innovation. This can come from government grants, private investments, or crowdfunding. Adequate funding supports research, technology development, pilot projects, and the scaling up of successful initiatives.
3. **Incubators and Accelerators**: Incubators and accelerators that focus on civic technology and digital democracy can provide resources, mentorship, and support for startups and innovators working on MOTMSDD-related technologies and applications.
4. **International Collaboration**: Collaborating with international organizations and networks can provide access to a broader range of expertise, resources, and perspectives. It can also help in setting global standards and best practices for MOTMSDD.
5. **Public-Private Partnerships**: Forming public-private partnerships can lead to a more efficient allocation of

resources, risk-sharing, and the leveraging of private sector innovation for public good.

In conclusion, Section 6 of Chapter 7 highlights the importance of fostering collaboration across government, private sector, academia, and civil society, and creating innovation ecosystems to support the development of MOTMSDD. Such collaborative efforts and nurturing of innovation are key to overcoming the technological, regulatory, and societal challenges of MOTMSDD, ensuring its evolution as a sustainable and effective model for civic engagement and democratic governance.

### Section 7: Addressing Societal Impacts

In Section 7 of "MOTMSDD: The Future of Civic Engagement," we address the crucial aspect of understanding and managing the societal impacts that arise from transitioning to a Metaverse Of The Minds Social Direct Democracy (MOTMSDD) society. This section delves into the strategies for managing these changes and ensuring that MOTMSDD is implemented in a way that is equitable and inclusive.

**Managing Transition:**

Transitioning to a MOTMSDD society involves significant social and economic shifts that must be carefully managed:

1. **Understanding Social Implications**: The shift to a MOTMSDD society will have profound implications on social structures, interactions, and norms. It is essential to study and understand these implications to prepare

society for the changes. This includes examining the impact on different age groups, communities, and professions.

2. **Economic Transition and Workforce Impacts**: The introduction of advanced technologies in governance and civic participation might lead to changes in the job market. There could be new opportunities in tech and data analysis sectors, but also potential job displacements in traditional sectors. Preparing the workforce for these shifts through retraining programs and educational initiatives is vital.

3. **Mitigating Negative Impacts**: Identifying potential negative impacts of the transition early on and developing strategies to mitigate them is crucial. This may include social support systems for those adversely affected by the transition, such as displaced workers or communities facing digital divides.

**Ensuring Equity and Inclusivity:**

An equitable and inclusive approach to implementing MOTMSDD is imperative:

1. **Addressing Digital Divide**: Ensuring that all segments of society have equal access to the technology and platforms used in MOTMSDD is essential. This includes addressing issues related to internet connectivity, affordability of technology, and digital literacy.

2. **Inclusive Design and Accessibility**: The MOTMSDD system should be designed with inclusivity in mind. This means making the platform accessible to people with disabilities, providing multilingual support, and

ensuring that the user interface is intuitive and user-friendly for all.

3. **Representing Diverse Voices**: MOTMSDD should be designed to represent and incorporate the voices of diverse groups, including marginalized and minority communities. This can be achieved through inclusive policy-making processes, community consultations, and ensuring diverse representation in decision-making bodies.

4. **Social Equity Policies**: Developing and implementing policies that promote social equity within the MOTMSDD framework is crucial. These policies should aim to balance the needs and interests of different social groups, ensuring that no group is disproportionately disadvantaged by the transition.

In conclusion, Section 7 of Chapter 7 emphasizes the importance of carefully managing the societal transition to a MOTMSDD society and ensuring that the implementation of this new model of governance and civic engagement is equitable and inclusive. By understanding and addressing the societal impacts, and by designing MOTMSDD systems that are accessible and representative of all societal groups, the transition can lead to a more engaged, empowered, and equitable society.

### Section 8: Conclusion: Embracing a New Era

As we conclude Chapter 7 of "MOTMSDD: The Future of Civic Engagement," it is imperative to encapsulate the journey towards embracing a new era of governance and societal interaction through the lens of Metaverse Of The Minds Social

Direct Democracy (MOTMSDD). This concluding section reflects on the key steps and strategies discussed throughout the chapter and issues a call to action for all stakeholders to actively participate in shaping this revolutionary future.

**Summarizing the Path Forward:**

The journey to a MOTMSDD future is paved with innovation, collaboration, and a commitment to societal betterment. The key steps and strategies outlined in this chapter provide a roadmap for this transition:

1. **Building the Technological Foundation**: Developing and refining technologies like BCIs, AI, and Quantum Computing is crucial for the practical implementation of MOTMSDD.
2. **Policy Frameworks and Governance**: Crafting supportive policies and robust governance models is essential to accommodate the innovative nature of MOTMSDD, ensuring ethical, legal, and societal alignment.
3. **Education and Awareness**: Educating the public and raising awareness about the benefits and challenges of MOTMSDD is fundamental in building trust and acceptance.
4. **Community and Individual Involvement**: Engaging communities and encouraging individual participation ensures that MOTMSDD evolves as a model that is inclusive and representative of diverse societal needs.
5. **Fostering Collaboration and Innovation**: Collaboration across sectors – government, private, academia, and civil society – and fostering innovation

ecosystems are vital for continuous development and improvement of MOTMSDD.

6. **Addressing Societal Impacts**: Managing the social and economic impacts of the transition to MOTMSDD, ensuring equity and inclusivity, and mitigating potential negative effects are imperative for a smooth transition.

**Call to Action:**

As we stand on the brink of this new era, a collective effort is required to bring the vision of MOTMSDD to fruition:

1. **Engage and Participate**: We call upon readers, citizens, policymakers, technologists, and all stakeholders to actively engage in the discourse and development of MOTMSDD. Your participation, feedback, and innovative ideas are the lifeblood of this evolving model.

2. **Embrace Change and Innovation**: The transition to MOTMSDD represents a significant change in the way we interact with governance and technology. Embracing this change, being open to innovation, and adapting to new ways of civic participation are key to realizing the potential of MOTMSDD.

3. **Contribute to a Collective Future**: MOTMSDD is more than a technological or political innovation; it is a societal shift towards a more inclusive and participatory future. Every contribution, be it small or significant, helps in shaping a future where every voice is heard and valued.

4. **Be an Advocate for Change**: Advocate for the adoption of MOTMSDD in your communities, workplaces, and social circles. Share the knowledge,

discuss the possibilities, and be a part of the movement towards a more direct and democratic future.

In conclusion, Section 8 of Chapter 7 not only recaps the path towards a MOTMSDD future but also serves as a rallying call for collective action. It is an invitation to embrace a new era of civic engagement, where technology empowers democracy, and every individual plays a role in shaping the societal fabric. The realization of a MOTMSDD society is a journey that requires the commitment, creativity, and collaboration of all, marking the beginning of a transformative chapter in the history of governance and civic participation.

---

## Conclusion

### *Section 1: Reflecting on the Journey*
As we reach the conclusion of "MOTMSDD: The Future of Civic Engagement," it is essential to reflect upon the journey we have undertaken, revisiting the key themes and insights that have shaped our understanding of the Metaverse Of The Minds Social Direct Democracy (MOTMSDD).

### Overview of the Book:

The journey through this book has taken us from the foundational concepts of MOTMSDD to the nuanced understanding of its potential to transform civic engagement and governance.

1. **Introducing MOTMSDD**: We began by introducing the revolutionary concept of MOTMSDD, a model that intertwines advanced technologies with democratic principles to create a new paradigm of civic engagement.
2. **Technological Underpinnings**: We delved into the technological backbone of MOTMSDD, exploring the roles of brain-computer interfaces, artificial intelligence, and quantum computing in creating an interconnected, responsive system of governance.
3. **Ethical, Legal, and Societal Considerations**: Our journey then navigated the complex ethical, legal, and societal challenges and considerations inherent in implementing such a transformative model.
4. **The Role of Policy and Governance**: We examined the necessary policy frameworks and governance structures that need to be established to support and sustain the MOTMSDD model.
5. **Public Participation and Education**: The importance of public understanding, education, and engagement was highlighted as a cornerstone for the success of MOTMSDD.

**Key Insights and Learnings:**

Each chapter of the book has offered significant insights into the multifaceted nature of MOTMSDD:

1. **Understanding MOTMSDD**: The initial chapters provided a comprehensive understanding of the MOTMSDD concept, highlighting its potential to revolutionize how citizens engage with and influence governance processes.

2. **Technological Advancements**: The discussions around the necessary technological advancements emphasized the need for continuous innovation and development in BCIs, AI, and quantum computing to make MOTMSDD a practical reality.

3. **Navigating Complexities**: Insights into the ethical, legal, and societal implications underscored the complexity of integrating such an advanced system into existing societal structures and the need for thoughtful, inclusive approaches.

4. **Policy and Governance**: The exploration of policy and governance revealed the need for adaptable, forward-thinking frameworks that can support the dynamic nature of MOTMSDD.

5. **Empowering Participation**: The book consistently emphasized the role of public participation, education, and community involvement as vital for the acceptance and success of MOTMSDD.

In conclusion, Section 1 of the Conclusion of "MOTMSDD: The Future of Civic Engagement" serves as a moment to reflect on the comprehensive journey we have taken. From conceptual understanding to practical considerations, the book has woven together a tapestry of ideas, challenges, and possibilities that define MOTMSDD. As we close this chapter, we are left with a deeper appreciation of the potential impact of MOTMSDD on society, governance, and the future of democratic engagement.

*Section 2: The Transformative Potential of MOTMSDD*

In Section 2 of the Conclusion of "MOTMSDD: The Future of Civic Engagement," we reflect on the profound transformative potential of the Metaverse Of The Minds Social Direct Democracy (MOTMSDD) in revolutionizing governance and civic engagement, and its capacity to empower individuals and communities.

**Revolutionizing Governance and Civic Engagement:**

MOTMSDD stands as a groundbreaking model with the capacity to fundamentally alter the landscape of governance and civic participation:

1. **Redefining Democratic Participation**: MOTMSDD offers a new paradigm in which democratic participation is not just about casting a vote but involves continuous, real-time engagement. This model enables a more dynamic interaction between citizens and their governments, where decision-making processes are more transparent, responsive, and reflective of the current sentiments of the populace.
2. **Enhanced Decision-Making Efficiency**: With the integration of advanced technologies like AI and quantum computing, MOTMSDD promises a leap in the efficiency of decision-making processes. Policies and regulations can be adapted more quickly to changing circumstances, and data-driven insights can lead to more informed and effective governance.

3. **Global Impact**: The potential of MOTMSDD extends beyond local or national boundaries. As a scalable model, it holds the promise of influencing global governance structures, fostering greater international cooperation, and addressing global challenges through a more participatory and inclusive approach.

**Empowering Individuals and Communities:**

At its core, MOTMSDD is about empowering individuals and communities:

1. **Direct Influence in Governance**: MOTMSDD shifts the power dynamics in governance, allowing individuals to have a more direct and immediate influence on decisions that affect their lives. This empowerment leads to a deeper sense of civic responsibility and engagement.

2. **Community-Driven Policies**: By leveraging digital twins and real-time data analysis, MOTMSDD enables policies that are more attuned to the needs and preferences of different communities. This approach ensures that the voices of all segments of society, especially marginalized and underrepresented groups, are heard and considered.

3. **Strengthening Social Cohesion and Equality**: MOTMSDD can strengthen social cohesion by fostering a sense of belonging and participation among citizens. When individuals see their input being valued and reflected in decision-making, it enhances trust in governance systems and nurtures a collaborative community spirit.

MOTMSDD advances equality by defining the goal of satisfying everybody's needs first and then addressing preferences and desires.

In conclusion, Section 2 of the Conclusion of "MOTMSDD: The Future of Civic Engagement" underscores the substantial impact that MOTMSDD could have on governance and civic engagement. It paints a picture of a future where governance is more inclusive, responsive, and efficient, and where individuals and communities are empowered to play a meaningful role in shaping their societies. As we envision this future, it becomes clear that MOTMSDD is not just a technological innovation; it is a transformative step towards a more engaged, empowered, and cohesive society.

### Section 3: Addressing the Challenges

In Section 3 of the Conclusion of "MOTMSDD: The Future of Civic Engagement," we focus on acknowledging and addressing the various challenges and hurdles identified throughout the book. This section emphasizes the importance of confronting these obstacles to fully realize the potential of the Metaverse Of The Minds Social Direct Democracy (MOTMSDD).

**Acknowledging Hurdles:**

The journey through MOTMSDD reveals a landscape filled with both promise and challenges:

1. **Technological Challenges**: We have identified significant hurdles in the technological realm,

particularly in the development and implementation of advanced BCIs, AI, and quantum computing. These challenges include technical limitations, ethical considerations, and the need for robust infrastructure.

2. **Societal and Ethical Considerations**: MOTMSDD raises critical societal and ethical questions. The ethical use of technology, data privacy concerns, and the potential for societal disruption are significant challenges that need careful consideration and management.

3. **Legal and Regulatory Frameworks**: Adapting existing legal and regulatory frameworks to accommodate the new paradigms introduced by MOTMSDD is a complex task. This includes creating new policies and regulations that are flexible enough to evolve with advancing technology while ensuring the protection of individual rights and societal values.

4. **Cultural and Behavioural Changes**: The success of MOTMSDD depends on cultural and behavioural shifts within society. Encouraging a transition to more active and continuous forms of civic engagement requires changes in public perception and behaviour.

**The Path to Overcoming Obstacles:**

Overcoming these challenges requires a multifaceted approach:

1. **Collaborative Efforts in Technology Development**: Collaborative efforts between governments, private sector entities, academia, and tech innovators are crucial for advancing the necessary technologies. This collaboration can lead to shared knowledge, pooling of resources, and more efficient problem-solving.

2. **Continuous Dialogue and Ethical Oversight**:
   Addressing societal and ethical challenges requires ongoing dialogue among stakeholders, including ethicists, technologists, policymakers, and the public. Establishing ethical oversight committees can help ensure that MOTMSDD develops in a manner that aligns with societal values and ethical standards.

3. **Adaptive Legal and Regulatory Structures**:
   Developing legal and regulatory frameworks that are adaptable and responsive to technological advancements is essential. This involves not only proactive policy-making but also the creation of mechanisms for regular review and amendment of laws and regulations.

4. **Public Education and Engagement**: Cultivating cultural and behavioural changes relies heavily on education and public engagement. Initiatives to raise awareness, educate citizens about the benefits and workings of MOTMSDD, and encourage active participation are vital.

In conclusion, Section 3 of the Conclusion of "MOTMSDD: The Future of Civic Engagement" highlights the importance of acknowledging and addressing the challenges identified throughout the book. Overcoming these hurdles is not a straightforward task, but with collaborative efforts, continuous dialogue, adaptive frameworks, and public engagement, the obstacles can be mitigated. The path forward requires commitment, innovation, and a collective will to transform the challenges into stepping stones toward realizing the full potential of MOTMSDD.

### *Section 4: The Role of Technology and Innovation*

In Section 4 of the Conclusion of "MOTMSDD: The Future of Civic Engagement," we focus on the central role of technology and the continuous need for innovation in realizing the vision of Metaverse Of The Minds Social Direct Democracy (MOTMSDD). This section underscores the enabling power of technology and the imperative of ongoing development to bring MOTMSDD from concept to reality.

**Technology as an Enabler:**

Technology is the cornerstone of MOTMSDD, playing a transformative role in enabling this novel model of governance and civic engagement:

1. **Brain-Computer Interfaces (BCIs)**: BCIs are pivotal in MOTMSDD, bridging the gap between human cognitive processes and digital platforms. They enable direct interaction and communication between individuals and the digital representation of governance structures in MOTMSDD, making real-time participation and feedback possible.
2. **Artificial Intelligence (AI)**: AI acts as the analytical and processing backbone of MOTMSDD. It is instrumental in handling and interpreting the vast amounts of data generated by digital twins, ensuring that decision-making is informed, efficient, and responsive to the needs and preferences of the populace.
3. **Quantum Computing**: Quantum computing brings unmatched processing power, which is essential for the

vast computational demands of MOTMSDD. Its ability to handle complex simulations and data analysis at unprecedented speeds is crucial for the system's efficiency and effectiveness.

**Continued Innovation and Development:**

The realization of MOTMSDD depends not just on existing technology but on continued innovation and development:

1. **Advancing Existing Technologies**: There is a need for ongoing research and development to advance the capabilities of BCIs, AI, and quantum computing. This includes enhancing accuracy, reliability, accessibility, and ethical considerations of these technologies.
2. **Innovative Solutions for Emerging Challenges**: As MOTMSDD evolves, new challenges will emerge, requiring innovative technological solutions. This could involve developing new algorithms, improving data security measures, or creating more intuitive interfaces for public interaction with the MOTMSDD system.
3. **Collaborative Technological Development**: The complex nature of MOTMSDD calls for collaborative efforts in technology development. Partnerships between governments, academia, industry, and technology experts can lead to more holistic and robust technological solutions.
4. **Fostering a Culture of Innovation**: Cultivating a culture that encourages experimentation, creativity, and technological exploration is vital. Encouraging startups and researchers to engage with the challenges of MOTMSDD can lead to groundbreaking innovations and advancements.

In conclusion, Section 4 of the Conclusion of "MOTMSDD: The Future of Civic Engagement" highlights the fundamental role of technology as an enabler of the MOTMSDD vision. It acknowledges the necessity of continuous technological innovation and development to address the evolving challenges and requirements of this model. Embracing and fostering technological advancement is not just a requirement but a commitment to ensuring that the MOTMSDD vision becomes a viable, efficient, and effective reality, shaping the future of governance and civic engagement in the digital era.

### *Section 5: A Call to Action*

In Section 5 of the Conclusion of "MOTMSDD: The Future of Civic Engagement," we extend a call to action to readers, urging them to take an active role in the discourse and development of the Metaverse Of The Minds Social Direct Democracy (MOTMSDD). This section is dedicated to inspiring critical engagement, participation, and collaboration in shaping the future of this innovative model.

**Encouraging Critical Engagement:**

The book aims to not only inform but also to provoke thought and discussion about MOTMSDD:

1. **Forming Independent Opinions**: Readers are encouraged to critically evaluate the concepts presented in this book. It's important to consider the implications, benefits, and challenges of MOTMSDD from various perspectives and contexts.

2. **Discussion and Debate**: Engage in discussions and debates about MOTMSDD with peers, colleagues, and in academic or professional settings. Diverse viewpoints and critical discourse can lead to a deeper understanding and improvement of the MOTMSDD model.
3. **Reflective Analysis**: Reflect on how MOTMSDD might impact your life, community, and society at large. Consider both the potential positive outcomes and the challenges or ethical dilemmas it might pose.

## Participation and Advocacy:

Active participation and advocacy are crucial for the evolution of MOTMSDD:

1. **Community Involvement**: Get involved in community discussions or initiatives related to civic technology and digital democracy. Your engagement can help shape how such concepts are implemented at a local level.
2. **Professional Contribution**: Professionals in technology, law, governance, and social sciences are invited to contribute their expertise to the development of MOTMSDD. This might involve research, policy development, or technological innovation.
3. **Online Platforms and Social Media**: Use online platforms and social media to spread awareness about MOTMSDD. Sharing information, starting discussions, and connecting with like-minded individuals can foster a broader understanding and acceptance of this concept.

## Fostering a Collaborative Future:

Collaboration across various sectors and disciplines is key to realizing the MOTMSDD vision:

1. **Cross-Disciplinary Collaboration**: Encourage and participate in collaborations between technologists, policymakers, academics, and citizens. These collaborations can address the multifaceted challenges of MOTMSDD and lead to more holistic solutions.
2. **Innovation Through Partnership**: Seek opportunities for partnerships in developing and testing MOTMSDD technologies and frameworks. Partnerships between academia, industry, government, and community organizations can accelerate innovation and practical implementation.
3. **Global Cooperation**: Since MOTMSDD has the potential for global impact, international cooperation and dialogue are important. Engaging in global forums and networks can help harmonize approaches to digital democracy and civic technology.

In conclusion, Section 5 of the Conclusion of "MOTMSDD: The Future of Civic Engagement" serves as an invitation and a call to action for readers to actively engage with, participate in, and contribute to the development and realization of the MOTMSDD concept. It emphasizes the need for critical thought, active involvement, and collaborative efforts to explore and shape this innovative model of governance and civic engagement, encouraging readers to be a part of this transformative journey.

*Section 6: Closing Remarks*

As we conclude "MOTMSDD: The Future of Civic Engagement," Section 6 is dedicated to offering final reflections on this innovative journey and to inspire hope and vision for the future possibilities that MOTMSDD presents.

**Final Reflections:**

This book has taken us through a profound exploration of the Metaverse Of The Minds Social Direct Democracy (MOTMSDD) - a concept that intertwines advanced technology with the foundational principles of democracy to envisage a new era of civic engagement.

1. **Embracing Change and Adaptation**: One of the core themes emphasized throughout this book is the importance of adapting to and shaping emerging technologies and governance models. As we stand at the cusp of significant technological advancements, our willingness to embrace these changes and adapt them for the betterment of society is crucial. MOTMSDD represents not just a technological leap but a fundamental shift in how we perceive and participate in democratic processes.

2. **The Role of Collective Effort**: The realization of MOTMSDD requires a collective effort from technologists, policymakers, academics, and citizens. It is a collaborative journey that demands open-mindedness, continuous learning, and a shared

commitment to harnessing technology for the public good.

**Inspiring Hope and Vision:**

As we close this book, we look forward to the transformative possibilities that MOTMSDD holds:

1. **A More Inclusive ,equalitarian and Participatory Future**: MOTMSDD opens the door to a future where civic engagement is not only more inclusive but also more participatory. It allows for a democracy where every voice is heard and every opinion matters, breaking down barriers and creating a platform for true representation.By using the satisfaction of everybody's needs as a welfare tool for public decision-making we improve socioeconomic equality.

2. **Responsive and Dynamic Governance**: With real-time data and continuous citizen participation, governance can become more responsive and dynamic. MOTMSDD has the potential to make policies and decisions that are timely, data-driven, and reflective of the current needs and aspirations of the populace.

3. **Empowering Communities and Individuals**: At its heart, MOTMSDD is about empowering communities and individuals, giving them the tools and platform to actively shape their society. It's a vision of a world where participation in governance is as integral and seamless as any other aspect of daily life.

4. **A Vision of Hope**: The journey towards a MOTMSDD future is filled with challenges but also immense possibilities. It is a path that leads towards a more engaged, informed, and empowered society. As we

navigate this journey, let us hold onto the vision of a world transformed by the power of collective will and technological innovation - a world where democracy is rejuvenated and reimagined for the benefit of society.

In conclusion, Section 6 of the Conclusion of "MOTMSDD: The Future of Civic Engagement" serves as a reminder of the transformative potential of MOTMSDD and a call to embrace the possibilities it holds. It is an invitation to be a part of a future that is more inclusive, responsive, and participatory, inspiring readers to contribute to the realization of this visionary model of governance and civic engagement.

## Appendices

### Appendix A: Glossary of Key Terms

The purpose of this glossary is to provide readers with clear and concise definitions of specific terms, acronyms, and concepts used throughout "MOTMSDD: The Future of Civic Engagement." This alphabetically organized list will aid in better understanding the content of the book.

**Artificial Intelligence (AI)**: A field of computer science dedicated to creating systems capable of performing tasks that typically require human intelligence. Examples include decision-making, visual perception, and language understanding.

**Brain-Computer Interface (BCI)**: A technology that enables direct communication between a brain and an external device, often used to assist, enhance, or repair human cognitive or sensory-motor functions.

**Data Privacy and Security**: Refers to the protection of personal data from unauthorized access, use, disclosure, disruption, modification, or destruction, ensuring confidentiality and integrity.

**Digital Twin**: A virtual replica of a physical entity, used in the context of MOTMSDD to represent individuals in the digital realm, encapsulating their preferences, needs, and opinions for decision-making processes.

**Direct Democracy**: A form of democracy in which people decide on policy initiatives directly, as opposed to a representative democracy where they elect representatives to make decisions on their behalf.

**Machine Learning (ML)**: A subset of AI that involves the development of algorithms which enable computers to learn from and make predictions or decisions based on data.

**Metaverse**: A collective virtual shared space, created by the convergence of virtually enhanced physical reality, augmented reality, and the internet.

**MOTMSDD (Metaverse Of The Minds Social Direct Democracy)**: An innovative governance model combining the

Metaverse, BCI, AI, and Quantum Computing to represent every citizen with a digital twin in the metaverse for public decision-making.

**Quantum Computing**: A type of computing that utilizes quantum-mechanical phenomena, such as superposition and entanglement, to perform operations on data, offering potentially exponential increases in processing power for certain problems.

**Real-time Democracy**: A concept within MOTMSDD where decision-making processes occur in real-time, allowing immediate participation and response from citizens.

This glossary serves as a tool for readers to navigate the complex concepts and terminologies used in discussing MOTMSDD, enhancing their understanding of the transformative potential of this model in civic engagement and governance. Each term, defined in the context of the book, provides a foundational understanding of the intricate dynamics of MOTMSDD and its implications for future governance models.

---

**Appendix B additional resources for further exploration of the topics related to MOTMSDD, the following resources are recommended:**

**Books and Academic Papers on Digital Democracy**

1. **"Digital Democracy: How Technology Is Reshaping Democratic Processes"** - Explores the impact of digital technology on democratic processes.
2. **"The Digital Divide: Arguments for and Against Facebook, Google, Texting, and the Age of Social Networking"** by Mark Bauerlein.
3. **"Consent of the Networked: The Worldwide Struggle For Internet Freedom"** by Rebecca MacKinnon - Discusses the challenges and opportunities of Internet freedom and governance.
4. **"The Net Delusion: The Dark Side of Internet Freedom"** by Evgeny Morozov - A critical examination of the role of the internet in promoting democracy.
5. **"Cyber-Democracy: Technology, Cities and Civic Networks"** - Examines the role of technology in enhancing civic engagement and governance.

## Documentaries on Brain-Computer Interfaces

- **"I Am Human"** - A documentary that explores the co-evolution of humans and technology, focusing on brain-computer interfaces.

## Organizations and Institutions

1. **Organizations in Brain-Computer Interface:**
    - **Neuralink Corporation** - Focuses on developing implantable brain–machine interfaces.
    - **OpenBCI** - A company dedicated to making brain-computer interface technology accessible to everyone.
2. **Organizations in Quantum Computing:**
    - **IBM**

- **Massachusetts Institute of Technology (MIT)**
- **Harvard University**
- **Max Planck Society**
- **University of Chicago**
- **Chinese Academy of Sciences**
- **University of California, Berkeley**
- **University of Maryland, College Park**
- **Princeton University**
- **Google Quantum Computer Research Centre**
- **University of Tokyo**
- **University of Science and Technology of China**
- **University of Washington**
- **University of Oxford**
- **Duke University**
- **National Institute of Standards and Technology**
- **Stanford University**
- **California Institute of Technology**.

These resources will provide readers with a comprehensive understanding of the various facets of MOTMSDD, including the technological, ethical, and societal aspects.